BARRON'S PARENTING KEYS

KEYS TO CHOOSING CHILD CARE

Stevanne Auerbach, Ph.D.

Director of the
Institute for Childhood Resources
San Francisco, California

D0839134

BARRON'S

New York • London • Toronto • Sydney

Cover photo by COMSTOCK INC.

Copyright © 1991 by Stevanne Auerbach, Ph.D.

All inquiries should be addressed to:
Barron's Educational Series, Inc.
250 Wireless Boulevard
Hauppauge, New York 11788

Library of Congress Catalog Card No. 91-2165

International Standard Book No. 0-8120-4527-0

Library of Congress Cataloging-in-Publication Data

Auerbach, Stevanne.
  Keys to choosing childcare / by Stevanne Auerbach.
    p.   cm. — (Barron's parenting keys)
  Includes bibliographical references and index.
  ISBN 0-8120-4527-0
  1. Childcare—United States. 2. Childcare services—United States. I. Title. II. Series.
HQ778.7.U6A96   1991
649'.1—dc20   91-2165
                                           CIP

PRINTED IN HONG KONG
9 8 7 6 5 4

Dedicated to both
my daughter, Amy Beth Auerbach,
and
my mother, Jeanne Stockheim,
who inspired my efforts.

ACKNOWLEDGMENTS

The author wishes to express her appreciation for the excellent editing by Jane O'Sullivan and Judy Makover of Barron's and Jerry Kamstra, Director of the Henry Miller Library Big Sur, and for the proficient production of Stephanie Willett-Shaw of San Francisco.

I also express thanks to Amy Beth Auerbach, Jeanne Stockheim, and Dr. Judith Schwartz for understanding the value of this undertaking.

CONTENTS

INTRODUCTION

The combining of work with parenthood is a delicate and challenging task. The job requires all the resources, ingenuity, skill, good humor, and strength you can muster. Millions of parents are working or must return to work after their children are born. Others want to return to school or need some time to pursue personal responsibilities. Before they can do any of these things, however, they must see that their children are well cared for while they are away from home.

Some fortunate parents have friends or relatives living nearby to assist them in caring for their children in an informal and inexpensive way. Many do not and must look elsewhere in their community to locate childcare.

The aim of this guide is to help you find and choose the best care possible for your child. Using the guide may also help you find a suitable arrangement more quickly.

Choices vary. A caregiver may tend your child in your home, in a family childcare home, or in a childcare center. However, finding a good and convenient arrangement is not easy. Good childcare programs usually have long waiting lists, may be inconvenient to reach from your home, or may cost more than you can afford. Most communities fall short in providing enough good childcare services to meet the demand.

All parents in search of childcare seem to want the same thing—a secure place that will provide consistent quality care, learning opportunities, and values that do not conflict with their own. They seek a safe, attractive place staffed with sensitive and caring adults who have an ample and varied supply of teaching materials, toys, and equipment. Parents also prefer a sliding fee scale based on their ability to pay.

For many parents the search for childcare is only one of several personal and family problems. Eager to solve at least one problem as quickly as possible, they may settle for the first available childcare arrangement. One young mother told me how she had met a woman at the laundromat who said she would take care of her fifteen-month-old son. The woman had not had any recent childcare experience, but she had just lost her husband and thought she would enjoy having a young person to look after. The mother was anxious to begin a new job and gave the care of her child to the woman. The first few days the mother called during the day and everything seemed all right. But when she arrived at the end of the day to pick up her son, she noticed the baby's pants were wet and the baby was cranky and irritable long into the evening. One day, deciding to check on the situation, she dropped by and found the woman watching soap operas on TV while her son was unhappily parked in a playpen.

Because an unsatisfactory childcare arrangement can become as great an emotional problem and energy drain as finding the childcare in the first place, it is worth the time and effort to make a thorough investigation before choosing a childcare provider. Finding the situation that will make you and your child happy may take weeks of searching and visiting, but the quick solution is no solution if your peace of mind—or your child—suffers.

The information in this guide will assist you in selecting the best possible childcare services with the least amount of time and effort. Included are detailed checklists giving specific points to look for in each of the places you visit. The kind of realistic questions you should ask at different stages of your search are also included to make your job easier.

The information and suggestions given should help reduce your feelings of uncertainty in selecting the most appropriate childcare situation. However, only you can make the final decision based on the personal needs of you and your child.

I recall vividly the experiences I had when my daughter was a baby and I had to return to work. The balancing act between home and work was never easy, yet I learned from my experiences. I want to share these experiences with you to help you find the best possible childcare available in your community. Good luck!

Stevanne Auerbach, Ph.D.

1

~~~~~~

NATIONAL TRENDS AND ISSUES

Childcare has been a controversial subject for many years. During World War II, when women were needed in the workplace, childcare was actively supported by the federal government. After the war many women had to continue working for personal and economic reasons, but instead of continuing stable childcare services, the government closed many programs.

Not until the 1950s, when the National Head Start Program began, did the federal government once again support early childhood programs outside the home. With the great difference in standards, funding, and quality of programs from state to state, childcare became a confusing patchwork of services.

Over the last twenty years the number of working mothers has doubled. The number of places available in childcare centers and homes has not kept pace with this increase. By the year 2000 it is expected that more than seventy-five percent of all mothers with children under the age of ten will be in the work force. The number of quality childcare services will need to keep pace with the needs of the family.

The need for infant care, before- and after-school care, and school vacation care, as well as the need for other family support services, continues to go unmet. The issue of paid

4

family leave for parents has recently been debated in Congress.

Legislation for expanded public childcare has been introduced many times in Congress. Finally in 1990, a childcare and development block grant appropriation to states was passed by Congress. It authorizes funds for improvements and training.

You can contact the mayor, state legislator, or congressional representative in your area to obtain current information on government action. The referral agencies, state licensing agencies, and references listed at the end of this book give you specific organizations to write to for further information and suggest additional resource books that might be helpful. Your local public library and Department of Education and/or Social Services can provide you with other local resources.

Many varieties of childcare services exist now. Availability is improving as the types and number of services provided are increasing to respond to the needs of families. Childcare is often available to some employees through union activities, employer-supported activities, or through employee cooperatives. More businesses have become aware of the importance of providing childcare support services as a benefit to employees. Different methods include on-site centers, referral to community sites, or shared facilities with other companies. The number of employer-sponsored childcare centers is still quite small, though.

Perhaps the unmet childcare needs of our society will soon be adequately responded to at the national, state, and local levels through the combined efforts of government, business, and industry. In the meantime, parents bear the responsibility and challenge of finding the best possible childcare services.

2

~~~~~~

KNOWING YOUR NEEDS

You are now a parent or soon will be one. You are thinking about combining work or school with your new family responsibilities. If you are going to be away from your child at any time during the day or night, you will need childcare. The kind of childcare you choose will depend on where you live, what you can spend, the number of available spaces, the number of families who want the same services, and your own persistence in obtaining the best services. You probably have many questions. For example:

"What effect will working have on my child and me?"

"How much of my earnings will be left after childcare and other work-related expenses?"

"How much will I have to participate and become involved in a childcare program?"

"How will illness, either mine or my child's, affect my employment?"

These are just some of the concerns expressed by parents who are working, or are considering working. There are no easy answers to these questions, especially since every parent has his or her own special needs, motivations, desires, and specific problems to solve.

A friend or neighbor who has been able to look after your child may no longer be able to do so. Perhaps you are recently divorced and must return to work, or perhaps you want to complete your education. You may simply need to have some time to take care of personal interests.

Whatever you are doing now or want to do is important to you as a person. You may be discovering new talents and abilities or may be seeking ways to gain new skills. Perhaps you worked before your child was born and now want to update your skills. You may want to prepare yourself for a future opportunity.

Knowing what you want is very important. Childcare services will give you the chance to earn money, go to school, or respond to other personal issues. It can also provide important personal advantages and growth for your child.

During an extensive study of childcare, I interviewed hundreds of parents of all economic and ethnic groups who used a wide variety of family childcare homes and centers. Parents revealed to me their concerns about childcare. I learned from the study and from all of my work in the field that all parents need good, reliable, quality childcare in order to continue working or going to school.

One parent, a nurse, had a problem finding childcare at night. She finally made arrangements with a neighbor whose child was about the same age as her own. The neighbor took care of her child evenings in exchange for her caring for the neighbor's child on weekends.

Another mother who was going to college was worried that she would not be able to continue school because the childcare arrangements she had depended on for some time had broken down. She eventually located a service near the campus and, fortunately, was able to finish school.

Still another parent, a father who had just obtained custody of two young boys (ages six and seven), found the problem of after-school care was critical. The boys needed supervision until he came home from work. He was fortunate to find a nearby recreation program that provided after-school care.

In each of the above cases, the parent's needs were different, and the solutions differed according to the individual situations. To determine your childcare needs, consider the following:

1. Will I need childcare every day?
2. During what hours will I need to leave my child with a caregiver?
3. How flexible are my hours?
4. Do I have alternatives, backup measures in case of illness or exceptions to daily routines, or must I rely solely on the childcare service?
5. What are my transportation needs or restrictions?
6. What are my financial limits for childcare fees?
7. What are the ages of my children?
8. Do my children have special needs?

3

MOTHERS AT WORK

The American mother with two children devotes at least 100 hours a week to the family, or 5200 hours a year, according to recent estimates. If she were paid, it has been estimated by the Harvard Insurance Group that her salary would be a minimum of $20,400 a year. Other estimates value her services at more than $40,000 a year.

When one realizes the many services a woman performs for her family, it is evident that her value to the family is very high. Although there is an increase in the number of men who share in the responsibilities of the home, in practice the main responsibility still rests with the mother. Even after she returns to work, either part- or full-time, many of the chores remain with the mother. For her continued well-being and that of her family, it is important for parents to discuss ways to share the responsibilities for the home and the children. Some of the responsibilities that have to be included are cleaning, shopping for food and clothing, medical appointments, sewing, dry cleaning, laundry, and home repairs. If you are a single parent, you may be able to share some of these responsibilities such as food shopping with another single parent who lives nearby.

During a study I conducted of childcare services and parents' needs one of the teachers I spoke to said she was unhappy while she stayed home during the first few months after her child was born. She had to earn money and was unable to use the skills for which she was trained. She felt somehow that if there had been flexible part-time hours or if she could have shared the job with another teacher, it would have allowed her to be a satisfied parent at home.

Another woman who was divorced when her child was three years old found returning to work an absolute necessity. She found a well-paying secretarial job and studied to brush up on her skills in accounting. Now she works as a book-keeper. A nearby childcare arrangement allowed her to improve her life and the life of her child. Most working mothers report that if they find the right situation for their child, their family life becomes more stable, productive, and dependable.

Many divorced mothers told me how much better they felt about themselves, their strengths and abilities, and their children's ability to cope with changes after they had successfully solved the problems of finding a job and a satisfactory childcare situation.

Some parents report that, as a result of having childcare available, their personal situations improved. They felt better about their ability to care for and support their families. One mother who felt particularly stressed and was not able to cope with her personal needs, saw that after she began utilizing childcare services, she functioned better in both her personal life and at her part-time job.

Some parents find childcare essential to their economic well-being. Studies show welfare rolls are reduced and the average income is raised with the parents' higher earning power, work stability, and lower turnover rate. Childcare is an important service that provides on-going support to the family and many benefits to the community at large.

4

‸‸

EFFECTS OF CHILDCARE ON THE CHILD

Y ou can reduce the worry that being away from your child during the day will be harmful to the child if you first take steps to prepare the child and yourself for the change. You will have to arrange meals, house-cleaning, and your personal needs carefully around the more limited time you will have. You also will want to set aside time each day to talk, play, and read with your child.

As you take on new responsibilities, your children will want to participate and assist you if you allow them to do so. Teach them to pick up their toys, clothing, and other personal belongings. Children can help set and clear the table and can help with light housekeeping chores, such as dusting. Children respond to the challenge of responsibility, especially if they understand the importance of their contribution to the family.

Individually, children vary greatly but in general all children have certain growth patterns. The child is most dependent up to two-and-a-half years of age. A child of this age group needs a stable individual to provide reassurance and continuity in care. If the child is two or more, he needs freedom to move around and be active, so that the best program for him at that age balances flexibility with firmness. At age three, when children are taking the first steps toward establishing their own individuality, it is important for them to be in situations that allow free expression within definable limits, particularly in regard to attitudes toward play, creative activities, and the use of equipment.

Tommy, for example, an only child, at one and a half needed a completely secure and stable situation. His mother found a family childcare home within a few blocks of their home, which fit his needs perfectly. She was able to give him the comfortable feeling that he was close to home and in familiar surroundings. On the other hand, Jane needed to be with other children in her age range, two or two and a half, and she needed more exciting activities while her mother was busy with the new baby. The half-day program she attended fitted her needs exactly. She was able to make friends, gain social skills, and find many outlets for her energy.

Three-year-old Johnny expressed the need to play with boys his own age. The childcare center near his home was the perfect solution for him. Other children, at four or four and a half, develop new skills more easily and adapt better to school the following year if they have had at least a half day of childcare or nursery school. Almost all children who have attended a nursery school or a childcare center find adjustment to kindergarten or first grade much easier.

Children in childcare situations benefit from early stimulation, which contributes to mental and social growth and development. Children who would otherwise be alone for the better part of the day find playing with other children builds their self-confidence and their ability to relate to others. Most children benefit from the opportunity to meet and be with children from different backgrounds. Many mothers reported to me their children learned many useful skills and were happier and more confident as a result of being in childcare.

Childcare also has drawbacks that you must consider before moving ahead with any plans. Some children are not going to be comfortable, join in, or adjust easily to their mother leaving them each day. This may be because of a lack of experience coping with separation—both on the parent's part and on the child's. Before making the childcare transition help your child adjust by providing experiences where he or she gradually learns to handle being with new adults and children.

5

^^

KNOWING YOUR CHILD

The first step in knowing about your child's needs is to think about your child's personality and how he or she responds to other children or adults. Is your child ready to cope with the change from home to childcare at this time? If not, you will want to assist your child in making the transition by providing opportunities to visit at a relative's or friend's home, or by making arrangements with a caregiver your child knows.

How would you describe your child? If your child is quiet, it would be best to start with a gradual program that will not push him or her to enter into too many activities. If your child is outgoing and self-confident, a childcare center that is more active and has a broader program would give him or her a variety of new friends. If your child is not toilet trained, he or she will feel more comfortable if personal attention can easily be obtained. If your child has a special health problem, a childcare home can often be found to meet those special needs. Check with local childcare referral agencies to locate one in your area.

Certainly, your child needs contact with adults other than yourself before attending a childcare center. He needs to feel comfortable with other adults and have the experience and confidence that when you leave him you will come back to him. Children learn to adapt to different situations at different rates. You will need to be sensitive to your child's reactions. You can help your child to respond favorably to new people by talking to him about visitors before they come to your home or about people he is going to visit. The more experience the child has being away from you, the more easily he will adapt to childcare. Teaching your child self-help skills, such as tying his shoes and putting on and taking off his own clothes, helps build confidence and ease around other children in a group setting. The more children feel good about themselves, the more they will enjoy contact with other children.

If you take pains to consider the special needs of your child, his or her unique personality and responses, your chances of working out a satisfactory arrangement are greater. It is important to generally know the families of the other children to know whether your child will fit in with the group. Cultural values, economics, and social compatibility make a difference in acceptance for your child and friendships for everyone.

For those children who will need some extra time to make the transition from home to childcare, an individual caregiver or a family childcare home with only a few children is usually a good first step. Other children who have had many chances to be away from their parents can function well in larger groups. They would find it challenging and would enjoy the wider number of activities offered by a large center.

As you visit each childcare place, ask yourself these questions about how it might meet your child's needs:

1. How much individual attention does my child need?
2. Will my child be comfortable and secure in this place?
3. Who are the adults and how will they respond to my child?
4. How will my child fit into this group of children?

5. How much does this place feel like home?
6. What will be expected of my child?
7. What are the staff attitudes about child rearing?

Your thoughtful review of each place will give you the best possible chance to locate the kind of care that will meet your child's needs.

6

~~~~~~

CARE OF THE INFANT

I t has been reported that thirty percent of women returned to their jobs when their children were less than six months old. Most had been able to arrange for childcare by caregivers or relatives in or near their home.

A great deal of controversy has centered on the appropriate age for leaving a child at a secondary home location. Most mothers find the adjustments are much easier when the child is at least three or four months old. Whatever the age, the child should have a consistent caregiver. Infants become used to a certain tone of voice and manner of holding; the caregiver, in turn, learns to recognize the infant's cues for distress, hunger, and playfulness. A baby is particularly sensitive and needs a great deal of loving, affectionate care. For infant care, family childcare homes where one individual is in charge are the best choice. If the mother feels comfortable with the arrangement and the baby is doing well, there should be no cause for concern.

If you have a caregiver in your home, you may have no more guarantee of quality care than you would if your child were in a family childcare home, a caregiver's home, or a center specially designed for the care of infants. However, the quality of the supervision, training, and other benefits obviously will be greater in those places designed and licensed specifically for infants.

In assessing a childcare center, you should look for:

1. A small number of infants with each adult
2. Caregivers who interact with consistent warmth and affection
3. A clean, airy place well designed for infants to play, move, and crawl about in safety (carpet, lighting, soft pillows, diaper-changing areas)
4. Active cooperation among staff who understand each other and the individual needs of the infant
5. Prompt and sensitive response on the part of caregivers to the various needs of infants (diaper changes, feedings, crying).

The characteristics you will want to look for in the caregiver are patience, warmth, and a nurturing attitude toward infants. The caregiver should be a person who likes infants and recognizes their need for communication, being cuddled and allowed to crawl about. The caregiver should be in good health and have the energy and interest to provide the balanced care so vital to a young baby. The program should offer sufficient individual attention, feeding, diapering, time for sleeping, affection and stimulation, and provisions for emergency care. The staff should encourage verbal and motor development on a continuous and consistent basis.

Children's needs change rapidly from birth throughout their early years. The more the caregiver knows and understands these needs, the greater the likelihood the program will promote your infant's growth and well-being.

7

PROS AND CONS OF CHILDCARE

Research has shown that quality childcare can have many benefits for the child. Children gain in independence; they learn to read sooner, develop new self-help skills, and converse more easily with others. They also have a good understanding of their parents' roles.

One mother reported her child, who whined and complained at home about not liking many foods, soon found he enjoyed the variety of foods offered at the childcare program. Another mother, who was concerned about her child learning to read, found the patience the caregiver had when talking to the child and reading books to him prepared him for easily recognizing words.

Children who have the opportunity to play and interact with other children grow in their ability to get along with others. They learn games and activities they may not have the opportunity to learn otherwise. As children interact and play with others, they grow in self-esteem and confidence.

Children of divorced parents who do not see their fathers frequently benefit from interaction with male teachers in some childcare programs.

Childcare provides other essential needs outside of the obvious ones. One mother, a lawyer, told me that her son, age four, had changed from being a shy and introverted child to one with enthusiasm and joy as a result of being in childcare. He was proud of each day's accomplishments, and his mother knew while she was preparing herself for future responsibilities her son was also.

A divorced father told me his children were better able to cope with the changes in their lives because of the encounters they had at the childcare center with other children of divorced parents. The father gained comfort by talking over issues regarding the childcare center with parents in a similar situation. Particularly, he was relieved when his daughter, age three, appeared less sad after she joined the program. By meeting other children and expressing herself openly, she became a more secure and happier child.

Other advantages of childcare for parents include the chance to talk to other parents and professionals about their children's behavior. Parents can also expand their social relationships. Many mothers mentioned the advantages of the discussion groups provided by the childcare center. Others were able to develop a parent cooperative for care during weekends. Still others formed a network of caregivers. Parents felt less isolated, made new friends, and had more ideas and resources to draw upon.

Some of the reasons given for not using childcare (and not working) are not applicable to anyone who must work for economic reasons. Certainly the choice is not always available. Feeling guilty about being away from your child doesn't help when having to face the reality of financial responsibility.

Of course, there are some disadvantages to childcare. And it is important to examine the pros and cons before plunging ahead.

Your child will form attachments to the caregivers. If something happens to the caregivers, the child will be affected. If the caregivers are not responsible people, your child could be exposed to problems that will have to be handled quickly by you. For example, a person who does not like children may ignore your child or not do appropriate child-development activities. Problems, when they do arise, can be difficult to deal with. That is why it is essential that you check credentials and personal references carefully. Your child may cry when you leave or ignore you when you get together later in the day. The adjustments are not always easy for the child or for you.

There are some disadvantages that you will not be able to avoid. You will not be around when your child makes a new step in her development—walking, riding a tricycle, making a great picture, or a construction—or when she just wants to talk with you about something special. Separation can be hard on the child and on the parents. But many of these obstacles can be overcome with understanding and communication. Some additional suggestions for handling problems that may arise are given in Key 41, Knowing Your Child Is Happy.

You will have the opportunity to weigh both sides of the issue and will hopefully select the best type of program to fit your own needs and those of your child.

8

▲▲

WHAT ARE THE CHOICES?

The three basic types of childcare arrangements are:

1. In-home caregiver (nanny, au pair, friend or relative).
2. Family childcare home.
3. Childcare center.

An **in-home caregiver** is an individual who is hired to take care of your child in your home for all or part of the day. Sometimes a caregiver is a relative or a friend who serves without pay. More often they are employees who receive a salary. The caregiver may be a nanny, an au pair, a babysitter, a student, or a retired teacher. In-home caregivers can be a convenient, but expensive, choice. To help keep the costs manageable, some families make *shared-care* arrangements. In shared-care, two or more families hire a caregiver to care for their children in the home of one of the families.

Family childcare is provided in homes set up to care for from two to twelve children. Such a home setting is the most common type of childcare outside the home. The providers of family childcare homes have modified their homes to fit the needs of small groups of infants, preschoolers, or school-age children. The number of children in the home varies. State laws typically require that no more than six children under age six, including the caregiver's own children, or only two children, if under age two, be cared for in the home at one time.

Childcare centers provide childcare for groups of from 10 to 100 or more children. Some centers offer childcare for both infants and preschoolers, but most provide care for pre-schoolers only. Some also offer after-school care. Centers are located in schools, churches, recreation centers, or in sepa-rate buildings. They usually have outdoor play space or a park nearby. Childcare centers may be privately run or sponsored by the government, churches, community organizations, em-ployers, unions, or other groups. The programs are usually run by teachers, who have had specialized training in early childhood education.

In the keys that follow you will find more detailed in-formation about in-home caregivers, family childcare homes, childcare centers, and other alternatives. The advantages and disadvantages of each will be discussed, as well as the specific qualities to look for in the different types of childcare ar-rangements. We will also provide you with checklists to help you organize your search and compare options.

You will want consistent, accessible, reliable, and af-fordable childcare services no matter which type you even-tually choose.

Consistent.   Will this be someone or someplace you can count on to take good care of your child, day after day, for an extended period of time?

Accessible.   Will this be someone or someplace you can get to without too much difficulty in terms of time, distance, and expense? Do the hours coincide with your schedule?

Reliable. Will you be able to trust the caregiver or child-care staff with your child's safety and well-being? Will they be where you need them when you need them?

Affordable. Will this be someone or someplace that will charge you no more than what you can reasonably manage within your budget?

The cost of childcare varies from $3 an hour to $6 or more an hour, or from $1500 a year to about $5500 (or as high as $25,000). The average cost tends to be close to $5 an hour or $5000 a year. For a live-in caregiver or nanny salaries generally range from $500 to $1500 per month, but can go as high as $2500 or more a month. Licensed infant center programs can be as high as $200 per week, toddler programs are up to $125, and preschooler care is from $100 to $200 per week. You can plan to deduct a part of your childcare costs from your federal taxes. Check with an accountant for the current information on exemptions and forms.

In some state-sponsored programs childcare can be free or at nominal cost for some, or it can be expensive, depending on your situation and the number and ages of your children. The amount you have to pay does not always indicate the quality of the program. Don't assume the more expensive program is the better one. Be sure to investigate low-cost or free options such as parent cooperatives or playgroups.

9

〽〽〽〽〽〽〽〽〽〽〽〽〽〽〽〽〽〽〽〽〽〽〽〽〽〽〽〽〽〽〽

ABOUT IN-HOME CAREGIVERS

Caregivers who live in your home go by several names. Some are called *nannies,* others are called *au pairs,* and still others are simply called *sitters.* Many nannies have had specific training and experience and are an excellent choice. Some young women decide to do the work of a sitter, nanny, or au pair for short-term experience and may not have had any training or previous experience. Sometimes in-home caregivers provide services such as light housekeeping or cooking in addition to their childcare responsibilities.

The in-home caregiver provides care, guidance, and mental stimulation in your home in a warm, loving, and patient way. The person you select must be knowledgeable about child development and how children learn, and should be able to plan appropriate activities for your child. If the caregiver will be working without supervision in your home, you must be very cautious. You will want to check references and take careful note of the personality traits of the person you are considering.

In-home caregivers usually are paid by the hour or week. Federal law requires that caregivers who work more than ninety hours a month receive the current minimum wage of $4.75. Experienced nannies, however, may charge up to $500 or more per week.

When you hire an in-home caregiver, you become an employer. You will have to pay your share of the Social Security tax and maybe your employee's share as well, depending on the arrangements you make. You may also have to pay unemployment, disability, and workmen's compensation insurance. Check with the Internal Revenue Service or your personal accountant.

If you are considering hiring a person who is not a United States citizen, you should consult an immigration lawyer to obtain the most current information on work permits, visas, and regulations.

Why choose an in-home caregiver? If you have two or more children, you may find it is less expensive to have them cared for in your home. Your child will benefit from having more individual attention. You will save transportation time and the inconvenience of getting your children to and from childcare arrangements. And, with an in-home caregiver, there is no need to make special arrangements when your child is ill. Also, your child will have less exposure to communicable diseases than at a family childcare home or a center. If your child is under five, or has any special physical or emotional problems, he or she may feel more secure at home. Since the caregiver comes to your home, the child does not have to adjust to a new setting. For the older child, being at home means being in his or her own neighborhood, near friends, and in familiar surroundings. If you work at night, a caregiver in the home is preferable, as the child cannot easily be taken out of the home at night, and outside care is hard to find after 6.00 P.M. The flexible hours an in-home caregiver can usually offer also help when you have an early or late meeting, or have to be out of town for a few days.

Probably the biggest drawback to having an in-home caregiver is the cost, which is generally higher than other types of care. Good in-home caregivers are also hard to find. And there is also the risk involved in depending on one person who may or may not show up on any one day. When the caregiver is ill, or her car will not start, or the roads are bad, or her own child is ill, you will have to make back-up arrangements quickly. The personalities of the child and the caregiver (or the parent and the caregiver) may be in conflict. Another important disadvantage of in-home care is the lack of group activities and stimulation from being with other children. In-home caregivers are not currently regulated by states, and with no one at home to supervise the caregiver or to see how the caregiver treats your child, it is often difficult to determine the quality of care.

The relatively high expense and limited availability of in-home caregivers makes this the least used form of childcare.

10

ABOUT FAMILY CHILDCARE HOMES

Family childcare provides a homelike atmosphere in which a group of children who are the same age or all different ages are cared for. The care is provided by adults, often mothers, whose child-training expertise can vary greatly, from those who have studied child development and have degrees in education to those whose experience is limited to caring for their own children.

There are two basic kinds of family childcare homes— small and large. A small home cares for six or fewer children, from infants through children of six years of age. A larger home can care for up to twelve children. The federal inter-agency guidelines recommend that two adults always be present.

Regulations for family childcare homes vary from state to state. In general, licensing regulations of these homes are aimed at safeguarding the child and do not necessarily specify the educational or social aspects of the program. Licensing homes does give you some protection, but does not always guarantee quality.

State, city, or county licensing most often assures you the home meets certain minimum standards of health and safety. Some regulations require personal qualifications on the part of the caregiver. Nevertheless, a license does not assure you the services provided will be satisfactory to you

28

or your child. Sometimes a home is not licensed because the regulations may require physical alterations in the house that the caregiver cannot make. Ask to see the license. Note the last time it was certified by a visit from the licensing agency. If the place is not licensed, ask why.

Be very careful if you are considering an unlicensed place. Federal, state, and local standards have been set up to protect the best interests of children by establishing the highest quality possible. Not having a license may indicate a serious deficiency not immediately apparent. A specific checklist of what to look for in a family childcare home is included later in this guide.

A family childcare home has many advantages. Most childcare homes are run by women who have raised or are raising their own children and have experience with and affection for children.

If your child is already in kindergarten or the primary grades, he or she may be cared for and supervised before and after school in such a home. If you have a preschooler the child may be in a group with other two-to-four-year-olds.

The family childcare home is usually best for a very young child or infant because of the close personal attention from the adults in charge and the homelike atmosphere. For the child who needs the warmth and the closeness of a small group of children, a family childcare home will probably be the best choice. Also, a home may be willing to care for a moderately ill child, while a larger center might exclude the child, forcing you to stay at home and lose days of work. A home also may be willing to provide care during odd hours, if, for example, you have a very early or a very late meeting. Another advantage is that often an older child can go there after school if it is near the child's school and home, which is more likely to be the case than with a center. The family childcare home is also usually less expensive than other types of childcare situations.

The disadvantages of a family childcare home must also be considered to avoid any problems. The caregiver may not be able to offer as many different and stimulating activities or play equipment as your child would have available at a center. With some caregivers, the children may spend too much time watching television. Caregivers in family childcare homes sometimes have less training in child development than their childcare center counterparts.

On the practical side, if the caregiver becomes ill, you may have to make other childcare arrangements on short notice. Coupled with this is the high turnover rate caused by burnout. Also children in a childcare home may lack contact with the variety of adults they would meet at a large center.

11

▲▲▲

ABOUT CHILDCARE CENTERS

Childcare centers provide care for large groups of children. They usually offer children a wide variety of activities, materials, and play equipment. They may provide breakfast and lunch as well as midmorning and midafternoon snacks. Naps and rest times are balanced with play and educational opportunities. Some centers take care of children before they go to school, some care for children after school, and some do both. Some care for preschool children only, for a half or full day. The staff is usually trained and knowledgeable, and follow a planned, suitable curriculum for the various age levels. Socialization skills such as sharing are taught as part of the curriculum.

The center is open during business hours to coincide with most parents' work schedules. Since there are several caregivers, and often backup caregivers as well, cancellation due to illness is not a concern. Although centers may vary in terms of staff, the sponsor, and the parents involved, most offer reliable care. Different agencies that provide childcare include nonprofit organizations such as YMCA's, church-related groups, colleges, universities, businesses, and for-profit programs, either independent or part of a chain or franchise.

Centers can also have disadvantages. They may be expensive or charge more than you can afford, or be difficult to reach from where you live. They may have too many children and not be able to give each child enough individual attention. Some children may not adjust easily to the size and school-like atmosphere of a center. Most centers make no provisions for sick children, which means you have to either stay home from work or make alternative arrangements if your child is ill. Since some centers only care for preschoolers, if you have an infant or toddler as well as a preschooler you may prefer a family home or an in-home caregiver so that you can keep your children together. If your work hours are not during the day, you may have to choose a family childcare home or an in-home caregiver willing to provide evening care.

Since most states require centers to be licensed, licensing of the center will give you an indication of the quality of the program. However, it does not ensure the quality. You still have to evaluate for yourself all of the aspects of the program. Keep in mind that states vary greatly in their minimum standards for childcare licensing. Because of this, when you request a list of the names and addresses of area childcare centers from your state licensing agency, request a copy of the state's licensing requirements at the same time. By reading the requirements, you will know what the minimal standards are in your state and how much store to put in the center's license.

What to look for in centers and how to find a center in your area are discussed in detail in later chapters.

12

‹‹

ABOUT OTHER ALTERNATIVES

Other arrangements for childcare exist, usually on a part-time basis, and are worth considering. However, most of the alternatives require parents' personal involvement and attention on an ongoing basis to make them work. If you can balance the time and conditions of participation with your other responsibilities, you could have an excellent arrangement.

A playgroup is one alternative. It is an informal cooperative operated and organized entirely by parents.

A playgroup is often the only inexpensive childcare available for infants and toddlers. The groups may operate on a rotating home basis, which works well if no more than five children are in the group and they are together for only a few hours each day. Sometimes a playgroup is formed when one parent exchanges childcare with another parent once a week. Other parents and children come to the playgroup gradually.

Parents have organized playgroups to provide care for as many as twenty children. Typically the parents hire a teacher to work along with each of the cooperating parents. The teacher provides skill, direction, and continuity to the group. If arrangements can be made for the group to meet with the teacher in the same place each day, services can be provided for more hours to more children. Hiring a regular teacher is often essential to large playgroup management.

One disadvantage of playgroups is the time and responsibility involved in their operation. If you have more than one child and must place your children in different groups because of their ages, scheduling playgroup time to coordinate with your work can quickly become complicated, and this arrangement can only work with part-time employment. Playgroup days are often disrupted when parents cannot show up as scheduled, and the whole group must readjust immediately. Problems such as deciding who is going to be responsible for what can slow down group meetings. Only if the parents have organizational abilities and sufficient time will a playgroup keep running smoothly.

The other major problem with playgroups is that sometimes the parents do not know what to do with the children during playgroup time. By sharing skills and creative energy, parents can provide a flow of good activities for young children during the day and learn the best ways to handle discipline. A playgroup means parents learning and working together.

Some playgroups deal with these various problems successfully. By visiting an established playgroup, you can get an idea of whether it will be suitable for you. Arrange to attend one of the group's meetings for more direct information, a feeling about how it operates, and to find out what the other parents are like. For the steps necessary to begin organizing a playgroup, I suggest you read *The Playgroup Handbook*, by Laura Broad and Nancy Butterworth.

A part-day program for preschoolers is a good alternative for children ages two to four and is often readily available. Half-day programs run either mornings or afternoons and are fine if you work part-time. They also help your child make the transition to time away from you. Programs of this sort vary in cost depending on the sponsoring group. Some are parent cooperatives with hired teachers and parents assisting in providing the program.

For many years the half-day programs have been recognized for the positive contributions they make to the child's early development. They have been the most widespread form of out-of-the home childcare and early education experience. Now, in response to the needs of working parents, some half-day programs have been extended to become full-day operations.

One of the most noteworthy of the part-day early childhood programs is Head Start, which is supported by the federal government. The Head Start program gives children the opportunity to have an early education that many parents normally could not afford.

If the part-day preschool is the only program near you with space available, you may be able to find someone to pick up your child at the school and to babysit for the remaining hours each day at your home or theirs. It can be a problem for your child to be in several different places during the day rather than having him or her in one safe, secure place. However, this arrangement can work if the segments of your child's day are scheduled carefully.

Pooling your resources with other parents is another alternative childcare arrangement, commonly referred to as *shared-care.* You may be able to join with another parent on a regular basis and work out an economical and effective arrangement. Together, you might be able to afford to hire the kind of caregiver you could not afford to hire individually. If an age difference keeps your children from being accepted at the same place, you can create your own family childcare home situation with another parent by employing a caregiver to come into one of your homes.

Childcare co-ops can also be an alternative. They are organized through churches, colleges or universities, large companies, and community organizations. Often they only emphasize occasional exchanges of services, giving you a list of students or other persons to choose from. Frequently it is hard to get a childcare co-op exchange going on a regular basis unless one person is in charge or unless the responsibility rotates according to an agreed upon schedule.

A communal living arrangement is yet another alternative if you and others agree to live together to share childcare. Living together can be a complicated problem or a simple solution, depending on the people involved. If you are well-matched and are willing to cooperate and share responsibilities, it can work out. The important thing is being able to talk freely to the person or persons with whom you will be sharing your child's care.

Family or friends may occasionally have the time and may want to make the commitment to raise your children as their own. More often, relatives and friends usually can offer only limited and sporadic help.

13

~~~~~~

AFTER-SCHOOL CARE

When children reach kindergarten or first grade, and through most of their elementary school years, their capacity for independence steadily increases. However, they still require supervision and attention. Many children, because of the scarcity of sufficient after-school arrangements, become "latchkey" children and return to their homes with no one there to greet and care for them. They are often lonely and have only a TV for company. It is not a good idea for children to consistently stay alone. Aside from being lonely, they may have problems with homework or fixing a snack, or they may be faced with a dangerous or frightening situation such as an accident, a fire, or an intruder.

Fortunately, many improvements are now taking place. More and more schools are staying open after 3 P.M. to provide interesting after-school recreational activities. Many family childcare homes, childcare centers, and youth groups also provide after-school care. Children at this age need a place to go, friends to play with, and engaging activities to occupy them. It is also a comfort to them to have an adult to whom they can turn. The availability of supervision after school provides for the needs of older children, allows them to study or play and gives them balance after school. A caregiver at home or shared between two families may be another good alternative.

At this age, children like dramatics, music, dance, crafts, art projects, games of all kinds, and sports. They like to be able to choose from a number of possible activities. Being part of a supervised group after school fills two needs, the need for security and the need for amusement while the parents are away. More communities are offering excellent after-school programs. These include parks and recreation programs, scouting, church groups, public and private schools, museums, libraries, and community centers. You can search for these programs through the resource and referral agencies in your area.

Be sure the adult supervisor understands children at this age, is sympathetic, supportive, reliable, and energetic. If you have a caregiver at home, it helps if they can drive, or travel easily with the child to the activities of interest. Trips can be planned for museums, libraries, the zoo, or other attractions in your area. To balance activities, the child needs time for quiet, homework, reading, or just listening to the radio or tapes.

Other activities for this age include gardening, sewing, hobbies, crafts, carpentry, computers, and creative writing. It is important to know the interests of your child and help him or her find ways to follow these special interests. These are the years when talent is discovered and nurtured through training and practice.

14

∧∧∧

BEGINNING THE SEARCH

The first step in choosing childcare is to look at your needs and the needs of your child. The next step is to search among the various arrangements possible. Use the specific checklists (later in the book) to make your decision. The choice you make will affect you, your work, and your child.

The feelings you have about the place and the people in it are important, but the feelings and experiences your child will have once in the arrangement are even more important. Adults can change jobs, classes, or personal relationships more easily than children. If you select carefully, making sure that your child's overall needs are met, the experience will be rewarding and positive for everyone.

Your first step in arranging childcare is to explore the options available in your community. Set aside a few hours one morning to make some preliminary telephone calls. You can get a lot of information over the phone without having to make a commitment.

To prepare for your morning phone calls, list phone numbers on a sheet of paper. Sources can come from the Yellow Pages, nanny agencies, parent newspapers, ads on bulletin boards, referrals from other parents, and other local services. See the the list of referral and state licensing agencies at the end of this book. In some lucky communities, one phone call to a childcare information and referral service will give you a lot of assistance. Quite often, such a referral service has a staff on hand five days a week answering parents' telephone inquiries about where to find childcare. Some also assist parents in setting up alternatives such as playgroups and small preschools. The referral service will give you current information on available centers, childcare homes, and other alternatives. The list they provide does not guarantee the quality of the programs. You will have to check the quality yourself by using the points given in the checklists in this book and your own intuition.

In most localities a state or county education or social services office has a listing of licensed childcare homes in your area. Since they usually are unable to give you the list the same day you call, call them a few days before you plan to make your morning phone calls. To reach the government department that provides this service consult your telephone directory. Look under the Department of Education, Public Welfare, Social Services, the Office of Family and Children's Services, Human Resources, or the Health Department. In some places, you can get a list of all licensed centers or homes in your area by calling the state or county health, social services, or education department responsible for licensing programs.

Other sources from which to gather phone numbers of possible childcare services are newspapers, school placement offices, bulletin boards, stores that sell children's products, community centers, and under Nursery Schools, Child Care or Day Care Centers in the Yellow Pages. Your pediatrician also might know of some childcare arrangements in your area.

Caregivers and family childcare homes often advertise in newspapers, so get both the large dailies and the smaller local weeklies. These people also advertise in local laundromats and on supermarket bulletin boards, so be sure to look there. However, many excellent caregivers or informal childcare homes rely on word of mouth and do not bother to advertise. Ask everyone you meet whether they know of any good childcare arrangements. Through a conversation in the park one day, one mother found an excellent caregiver who lived right across the street from her. An informal conversation between two other parents at the supermarket checkout counter led them onto the topic of caregivers. Through the chance referral made by one parent, the other found the perfect caregiver.

You may want to advertise yourself, using help-wanted columns or posting ads on local bulletin boards. Include as many details as possible in your ad. Carefully screen the candidates who reply to your ad following the suggestions given in this book.

Do not settle for the first person you find or the place that is nearest at hand even if appearances seem perfect. Check several situations so you can be certain you have found the best arrangement and you will have possible alternatives if you need them later.

The information you gather on caregivers, centers, homes, and informal alternatives may quickly become overwhelming and confusing. Keep all information in a notebook and make lists of phone numbers for each type of situation—caregivers, homes, centers, and any alternative arrangements you find. Organize the information in your notebook by location, cost, and type of service. Now you are ready to take the next step—obtaining specific information on each situation.

15

‸‸

INTERVIEWING ON THE TELEPHONE

One of the best ways to obtain specific information on different childcare arrangements is to make phone calls. Record the information you get in the notebook you are putting together on childcare. Your first conversation might go like this:

> "Hello. My name is_____. I have a job with
> _____and have a young child who is____
> years old. I am looking for childcare and would like
> to know if you have space in your program. Do you
> have time to talk about it now? Do you have an ap-
> plication form and can you send it please? Thank you
> very much."

You may still want to continue with your questions even if there are no openings, if the person has the time. You may keep this information for a possible opening later. Or the caregiver may ask you to call back when it is more convenient to talk with you.

Here are some questions to ask on the phone before you decide to visit.

1. Do you have a current license? Who licenses you? (If there is no license, find out why.)
2. How many children are you taking care of?
3. How many adults work there?

4. What hours are you open? When can the children come and when is pickup time?

5. How much do you charge? Do you have a sliding-fee scale?

6. Would you describe the building? Program? Activities? What is a typical day's schedule?

7. Do you provide any special services, such as transportation? Health care? Trips?

8. What are the meals like and who prepares them?

9. Who will be with my child? (If this is not already apparent.)

10. How does the caregiver or center handle individual differences in children (energy levels, interests, skills, and so forth)?

11. What are the special skills you have? Did you go to school for training to work with children?

12. Can I talk with other parents who use your program?

13. What arrangements are made in emergencies, such as an illness, to care for the children?

If your questions have been answered to your satisfaction, arrange a date and time to visit when you can meet the person who will have the most contact with your child and when the children will be involved in their usual activities. If a visit is not in order, thank the person for his or her time and continue through your list.

Sometimes the waiting list is very long, especially for a good program. This may be discouraging. If the program is what you want, however, it may be advisable to place your name on the list for the future. Sometimes a space will open up just when you are ready for a change anyway. A busy childcare center director or family home caregiver might discourage you from visiting until there is actually room in the program for your child. But if the program sounds excellent and it is convenient and possible to visit to find out what it is like, do so. Then you will be more certain about using the service later on.

16

~~~~~~

PLANNING A
WORKABLE BUDGET

C hoosing childcare is no simple matter. As we stated, the most expensive programs are not necessarily the best. Indeed, some of the best programs are the cheapest, if not free altogether. The costs depend on where the funds for the program come from—whether from the federal, state or local government, from the school system or the welfare department, from private foundations, religious groups, private industry, or entirely from contributions by parents.

Many good and accessible programs accept only the children of single parents or those on welfare. In these cases, your income may disqualify you from the program. Other programs have fee scales based on income. This may result in your paying a higher percentage of your income for childcare as your income increases, leaving you with less money after a raise than before.

You must establish your personal priorities clearly. Bear in mind the effect working will have on your child. Think about costs related to taking a job. If you receive food stamps and/or public assistance, consider the effect working will have on your eligibility for these benefits.

Before you commit yourself to work and childcare, consider alternative arrangements. Usually there is more than one combination of things you can do to meet your family financial responsibilities and pursue your study, job, and personal goals at the same time. It is a good idea to try to imagine yourself in each of the possibilities. For example, you could put your child on a waiting list for a center and find a part-time caregiver so you can enroll in a training program. You could participate in a parent co-op and work part-time. You could use the skills you have to take a job that is not entirely satisfying but that pays enough for you to afford childcare and to support your family until you can locate the kind of job you want.

It is important to consider exactly what your expenses will be so you will be prepared for them. Let's start by thinking through the expenses involved. Use this sample budget as a guide to list your alternatives.

BUDGET

EXPECTED INCOME	JOB A	JOB B	JOB C
Annual	_____	_____	_____
Monthly Gross	_____	_____	_____
Monthly Net (Take-Home)	_____	_____	_____

EXPECTED MONTHLY EXPENSES

Rent	_____
Food	_____
Utilities	_____
Medical	_____
Other Fixed Payments	_____
Costs of Childcare	_____
Total	_____

EXPENSES THAT VARY
DEPENDING ON YOUR LIFESTYLE

Transportation	_____
Personal	
Schooling	_____
Your Clothing	_____
Children's	
Clothing	_____
Meals Away	
from Home	_____
Entertainment	_____
Total	_____

17

~~~~~~

WHAT IS QUALITY CHILDCARE?

E very state has laws regulating family childcare homes and centers. They must be licensed, certified, or registered according to each state's laws. Although there has been some discussion about establishing a model state licensing code, not much has been done to implement this as yet.

Every center and home must have a license, although having one does not ensure quality. Ask to see the license when you go to visit. These licenses are meant to ensure that the center or home meets certain basic health and safety standards. Usually the licensing inspector visits the program before it begins operation and then is supposed to return for periodic follow-up visits and for license renewal. If the facility has funding from the federal government, then the federal interagency childcare requirements apply. The way to learn about childcare licensing requirements is to contact your state or county daycare office.

Childcare programs should always be more than just merely custodial. The childcare center or home, as suggested by the federal guidelines and state regulations, must offer a planned program of age-appropriate activities that provide for the mental, social, intellectual, and emotional development of the child. The daily programs must be described in writing. These planned activities must meet the developmental needs of the children.

Examples of daily scheduled activities that children should be able to count on are pleasant conversation among children and caregivers, ample opportunities for play (including outdoor play), time for rest, and flexible time for participation in a variety of projects (simple cooking, reading and looking at books, taking walks, playing games, and singing songs). (See Key 18, What Is a Typical Program? for more detailed information on what to look for.)

Another requirement for licensing is the provision of a variety of appropriate play materials. Older children must also have opportunities for play and exercise with supervision. Infants should have space to crawl about, and sufficient staff to hold, talk to, and feed them.

Centers are required to provide a trained, competent staff. Those who operate family homes, on the other hand, are frequently untrained but experienced. Many family home providers, though, have taken courses in areas related to early childhood education. More and more training of this type is being offered by colleges and universities with class schedules that fit the time constraints of family home caregivers. The purpose of training for both the center staff and other caregivers is to acquaint them with normal patterns of child growth and development and to ensure that they learn and sustain the skills necessary to respond to children's needs. Training for childcare center staff includes previous experience working with children, and appropriate specialized courses related to childcare. Training should include handling of behavior problems, ways of working with parents, nutrition and good eating, health, safety, and first aid, plus the design and use of space. In addition, courses in child psychology, enhancing learning for young children, use of toys and play things, and recreational activities should be taken. All of these are seen as factors that relate to the child's well-being in the program.

Federal guidelines recommend that childcare centers and homes provide nutritious meals and snacks, and that parents be given written menus for the week. In the area of health, the center should have a medical history of each child, including recent immunizations. The child should receive a health assessment from a pediatrician or family physician. Recent dental examinations are also recommended. The guidelines also recommend that the center have plans to respond to illness and emergencies, and that these plans be in writing. The guidelines suggest that parents receive information on health services available in the community as well as guidance in locating the right services. The staff should be trained in CPR and other emergency first aid skills. First aid equipment should be on hand. Lead-free paint should be used throughout the facility. There should be procedures for reporting suspected cases of child abuse and neglect.

The guidelines recommend parents have adequate opportunities to observe and discuss the children's needs. Parents must be informed about the program and be able to exchange information with other parents. Parents can communicate through periodic meetings together, observation sessions, conferences, and parent advisory councils. Parents should have opportunities to evaluate the program, review budgeting, and learn parenting skills at parent education classes. All information should be provided in the primary language of the parents. The guidelines recommend state agencies provide a checklist to aid parents in assessing the quality of childcare programs, and that the agencies establish procedures for parents to raise questions about the programs and provide information referral services to help parents locate childcare.

The standards for family childcare homes are also included in the federal guidelines. Standards should be considered minimum for any program you would consider for your child.

How the center or home establishes policy will affect you as a parent. You should pay close attention to the degree of responsibility, responsiveness, and caring shown by the staff and management. Observe the behavior of the children as they come to and from the program. Are they happy and satisfied? Do they look eager to be there? Watch how the staff interacts with each other, talking about the children and about what is happening. Do they seem interested, responsive, and involved?

Mealtime often gives a clue to the real quality of the program. It should be a sociable and relaxed time. Menus should be varied, nutritious, interesting, and appropriate for the age of the children.

Observe the quality of the toys, educational and recreational materials, and equipment used by the children. The space should be organized so the children are free to move around safe from accidents. There should be places to talk and to be private.

The staff's attitudes should be caring and nonsexist and should show a sensitivity to the children. There should be opportunities for the children to express their feelings, and for staff to deal with behavior problems in a constructive way. Attitudes should be positive and energetic. The children should enjoy being with each other, learn to cooperate, and be respectful to each other. The caregivers should talk to the children and to each other in an easy, comfortable way. They should work well together.

Most parents know instinctively when they have found the right place. Parents have told me they knew immediately, by the way the staff spoke and reacted to them, whether or not it was a good program. Equipment and facilities aside, the staff is the key to making a program work. To verify your reactions, I suggest you also talk with other parents who have been using the program.

18

∿∿

WHAT IS A TYPICAL PROGRAM?

G ood programs for children balance active pursuits with restful interludes. Depending on the staff and the ages of children, the basic elements of the program include: talking and sharing, indoor and outdoor play, arts and crafts, reading stories, and special projects. A program for pre-schoolers will include learning numbers, puzzles, games, music, cooking, and everyday living routines. Meals and snacks, naps, and clean-up time are part of most programs.

The following is a typical day's program in a structured setting, such as a childcare home or a childcare center. The specifics will vary from place to place. A caregiver would arrange her own schedule of activities.

MORNING

7:00 – 9:15	Free play, inside and out, snack time
9:15 – 9:30	Cleanup and bathroom
9:30 – 10:00	Group time, sharing and music
10:00 – 11:00	Various indoor activities, learning centers and projects
11:30 – 12:00	Story time and bathroom (cleanup and rest period)

AFTERNOON

12:00 – 12:30	Lunch
12:30 – 2:30	Nap
2:30 – 3:30	Getup, bathroom, and snack time
3:00 – 3:45	Arts and crafts, free play
3:45 – 4:00	Cleanup
4:00 – 5:00	Outdoor play
5:00 – 6:00	Quiet activities

On arriving, the children are greeted by the staff and made to feel welcome. They put their coats or sweaters in the storage unit; then, depending on the hour, they may have breakfast with the other children. Some programs give parents menus of the food to be served during the week so that they can plan their own menus at home accordingly.

The first session includes any number of activities geared to the age level and interests of the children. This is a time when some children will be working on specific skills, by learning through doing. Typical activities of this nature include storytelling, cutting out pictures, assembling puzzles, listening to records, dramatic play, growing seeds and plants, using art materials, making craft projects, play with blocks, learning shapes, experimenting with colors, and discovering movement through exercise or dance. Later, the children have time to go outdoors and play; sand, water, blocks, tricycles, and other toys make this time challenging and fun.

When the children return indoors for cleanup and rest before lunch, there may be music to listen to or quiet songs and stories. Lunchtime is always a major event and is an enjoyable time for everyone. Sometimes the children help to prepare the food. Making salad, Jell-O, cookies, or preparing fruits and vegetables are activities children enjoy.

54

Naps after lunch are vital to the children's well-being. While some merely rest quietly, most of them sleep during nap time.

After nap time and snacks, activities similar to those of the morning are often engaged in. For example, crafts, dramatic play, or making a snack are activities that children enjoy. Sometimes there may be an hour of quality children's television, but more often the time is spent playing and learning, indoors or out, perhaps constructing something from wood or other materials. In a good program television watching is kept to a minimum.

The entire program of the center or childcare home should reflect the combined efforts of the staff working cooperatively. The specific types of activities are limited only by the skill and imagination of the people who will be caring for your children each day.

The close of the day is as important as the beginning. Each child should feel the day was spent in a stimulating and satisfying way. Parents need to know about their child's progress and be made to feel welcome at the beginning, and end of the day—or at anytime.

19

^^

OVERALL QUALITIES
TO LOOK FOR
IN CAREGIVERS

C hildren need adults to listen and respond to them. They need to know they matter to adults and that their needs are important. They need guidance and help. Children like adults who are flexible, positive, and fair. Caregivers should never ridicule or shame a child or use harsh methods of discipline. All children need reasonable limits and to be treated with humor and common sense.

During your visit note how the caregivers respond after the child accomplishes a task. See if they treat boys and girls differently. There should be no discrimination in their attitude or behavior. Regardless of a child's ethnic background, they should respect the child's culture, language, and family values.

It is critically important the people working with children have no physical, emotional, or mental conditions that preclude them from working effectively, such as illness, hostility, or incompetence. They should have periodic X-rays and TB tests, and be free of all communicable diseases. They must have a working knowledge of first aid and emergency care. Records of each staff person's medical history should be on file in the childcare center's office. The caregivers must be emotionally stable and be positive in their attitude toward children.

The program should have a regular procedure for interviewing and screening potential employees. It is important to remember credentials alone do not insure quality care. Despite impressive credentials, some people may be unable to relate to small children or be consistent in discipline or they may have other shortcomings. Many caregivers without formal training are naturally responsive and loving with children and, with some special training, can become excellent caregivers.

Most programs understand the value of having a balance of male and female staff members. Children whose parents have been divorced or who lack a father's presence in the home, as well as others, greatly benefit from a balance of male staff.

Meeting with parents is extremely valuable for the staff. Even the most experienced professionals can gain from discussion with parents. The information parents provide enable staff to cope more effectively with special problems that may crop up.

The quality of the staff is critically important to the effectiveness of the childcare service. The equipment and facilities will vary, the food served will differ, but the most important aspect is who the adults are and how they relate to the children. Regardless of whether or not the program selected is in a home or center, the staff is the most critical aspect of the successful program. They must be loving, caring, and responsible adults. They should be able to help children to get along with others. They should be able to guide children in making new friends, sharing toys and other materials, and respecting the rights and possessions of others. They should give each child individual attention every day, praising each one, and seeing to their special needs. While being in control, they should still be loving and energetic. Caregivers must be people who are able to be fair and enthusiastic, and most of all, loving, caring and responsible.

Many different people work in childcare services. The director, who is responsible for the overall program, has training in childhood education, plus any special training necessary to qualify the person for a particular program, such as Montessori training. The teachers vary in skills, backgrounds, amount of training, and age. Their training is important, as is their attitude, their experience with children, and their personal philosophies.

The program may also include volunteers, such as students and senior citizens. Students need to have an opportunity to learn more about children and to have direct experience with them. High school students who volunteer in childcare learn many important parenting skills.

Many older persons enjoy participating at a childcare center, and they have rich experience to offer the children. Being with the children helps alleviate loneliness and gives them a feeling of contributing to their community. Having senior citizens and children together can work well for members of both groups.

Social workers may be employed by the center to help with problems that may arise with the families or with parents and their interrelationship with the staff.

Psychologists can be called for particular problems. Children can be referred to a child psychologist if a teacher and parent feels there is a need. Problems may arise from a traumatic or stressful event, such as a death or a divorce in the family. The child will benefit by having some attention to help him cope with the problem.

Other members of the community, such as designers and architects, community planners, contractors, and researchers, may be part of the board of advisors. Business and community leaders may be interested in childcare and also be willing to invest some of their time by serving on the program's board of directors.

Whether one considers childcare from the point of view of the baby, the toddler or older child, or from the parents' view, it is an enormously important community service. The involvement of all segments of the community ensures a higher level of service for everyone living and working there.

20

SPECIFIC POINTS TO LOOK FOR IN CAREGIVERS

The most important qualities of a successful caregiver are listed here for you to review when you make your visits or conduct interviews.

1. Are they able to talk easily with children?
2. Do they know about the special needs of each child?
3. Do they respond positively, sensitively, patiently?
4. Do they have a sense of humor?
5. Do they listen to the children and answer their questions?
6. Do they encourage each child to use his or her imagination and creative skills?
7. Are they competent in what they do?
8. Do they respect the individual and cultural differences of each child?
9. Do they create a warm and loving atmosphere?
10. Do they manage discipline without spanking, threatening, shaming, or hurting the child?
11. Do they allow the children to work out their differences and solve problems without too much interference?

12. Is there a personal awareness of how their moods, tone of voice, and behavior affect the children's behavior?
13. Do they respect each child and family and communicate easily with the parents?
14. Do they share and respect the parents' philosophies about children?
15. Do they assist each child in developing good health habits?
16. Do they express love to the children?
17. Do they respond to parents' needs and keep appointments on time?
18. Do they take time to explain details?
19. Do they seem happy to have parents visit and participate and do they encourage such participation?
20. Do they have knowledge of child development and select appropriate activities?
21. Do they seem to feel good about themselves and the job they are doing?

If you have a child that is an infant or below age three, the training and supervision will be better in a program that is specifically set up to care for infants. Here is a list of questions to ask yourself about the infant and toddler caregiver.

1. Enjoys being with babies?
2. Has patience, warmth, and a nurturing attitude?
3. Knows that infants need to be talked to and cuddled?
4. Is aware of their nutritional needs?
5. Provides space where infants can play and crawl?

6. Promotes active cooperation between parents and staff?
7. Knows how to handle emergencies?
8. Is in good health and has plenty of energy?
9. Provides activities that are stimulating and appropriate to the baby's age?
10. Understands and cooperates with the parents' efforts to toilet train?

If your child is age three to six, these questions are important to consider when selecting a caregiver.

1. Communicates with the child, talking, reading and teaching new words?
2. Responds to each child in a warm and loving way?
3. Respects the individual differences of the child?
4. Has positive self-image?
5. Is energetic and imaginative in choosing activities?

If your child is between age six and twelve, these additional questions are important.

1. Respects the child's need for both independence and dependency?
2. Is able to plan for and respond to the child's individual needs?
3. Respects the child's ideas and values?
4. Is willing to cooperate and sets clear limits of behavior?
5. Expresses a positive image for the child to respond to?

Of the many characteristics we seek in child caregivers the most important is that the caregivers listen to the child and respond.

You also will need to look at the number of children in the group in relation to the number of adults. There has been a lot of controversy about this ratio. The following guidelines are the recommended ratios of adults to children:

- Infant care is provided in groups of no more than 8 children, with 2 adults for each group of 8 children.
- Two and three-year olds are in groups of no more than 16 with at least 2 and preferably 3 adults for every group of 16 children.
- Four and five-year olds are in groups of no more than 20 children with at least 2 adults for each group of 20 children.

21

QUALITIES TO LOOK FOR IN ANY CHILDCARE ARRANGEMENT

Philosophies differ among child caregivers, and factors such as facilities and ages and numbers of children certainly differ from one type of childcare arrangement to another. However, basic issues are consistent, despite the variations. Regardless of setting, the points in the following list should be apparent in any program involving children.

1. A safe bathroom
2. A safe appliance area
3. Lead-free paint
4. Play areas clean and clear of clutter
5. A private rest area where sick children can be quiet
6. Safe childproof electrical sockets
7. Skidproof rugs
8. Personal non-breakable drinking cups, or paper cups
9. Consistent safety measures
10. Comfortable and cheerful environment
11. Enough space inside and out
12. Adequate supervision when children are outside
13. A nutritious and balanced menu
14. Snacks provided
15. Limits on or no "junk" food

16. Food not withheld as punishment

17. Same person takes care of child over a period of time

18. Programs offer interesting and stimulating daily activities

19. Group sizes are kept small

20. Routines are clear and predictable

21. Children participate in play as they would at home

22. Children are given choice of developmentally appropriate activities

23. Ample, varied materials provided for educational activities

24. An ample number of appropriate toys and play equipment available

25. Children expected to help put things away to the best of their ability

26. Television watching carefully selected and kept to a minimum

27. Nap time rules enforced

28. Balanced rest and play activities

29. A variety of interesting books are available

30. The caregiver reads aloud to the children

31. Children have been immunized

32. Working relationship is established with a health-care professional who provides appropriate care for sick children

33. Arrangements can be made for care during sick days

34. Care is provided on vacations and holidays

35. Emergency numbers are listed by telephones

36. First aid materials are handy
37. Caregivers are prepared to deal quickly and correctly with emergencies
38. Safety plans for emergencies such as tornados, fire, severe weather are established

22

SEARCH FOR A FAMILY CHILDCARE HOME

Once you have put together a list of potential places, you will want to get as much information as possible over the phone. If the person you call is too busy to answer your questions, arrange to call back at a more convenient time.

Have paper and pencil ready. Write down in your notebook:

1. The name of the childcare home
2. The address (cross-street helpful)
3. The telephone number

Then ask and put down the answers to the following questions:

1. What is the experience and training of the caregivers?
2. How long has the home been available for childcare?
3. How many children are being cared for?
4. Is the home licensed?
5. Is care provided if the child becomes ill?
6. What provisions are made for emergencies?
7. What information is kept on each child?
8. Are parents expected to participate in the program?

9. Can you have the names and phone numbers of the parents who use the home?

10. Can you visit the home? If yes, arrange a time to do so.

Note how long it takes you to get to the home and the distance traveled. Be prepared to give the caregiver your work schedule, phone numbers at work and other pertinent information. Observe the home's setting and how it relates to your views on childcare.

You will want to pay particular attention to the personal characteristics of the caregiver. You are looking for someone who has a positive awareness of children, is warm and affectionate, is consistent about setting limits, and knows how to respond to each child individually.

Ask yourself the following:

1. Does this person make you feel welcome?
2. How does she relate to the children?
3. Is she enthusiastic and positive?
4. Does she use positive methods of discipline?
5. Does she listen to the children?
6. Is she in good health?
7. Does it seem she would respond well in an emergency?
8. Does she have an understanding of child growth and development?
9. Does she respect the children?
10. Does she have an attractive personality?

Take a careful look at the physical environment. There should be plenty of space for free movement and activities.

The more attractive and comfortable the place is, the more positively the children will respond.

Indoors, ask yourself:

1. Is there enough space for children to play?
2. Is there a balance between active and quiet areas? (Children need places where they can be by themselves, to be quiet, study, or rest.)

Outdoors, ask yourself:

1. Is there enough space for children to play that is away from traffic and other dangers?
2. Is there a park nearby for more active play?

The overall quality of the home will depend on the person in charge and the staff. There should be enough adults to give the children the individual attention they need.

If the child care home receives state or federal funds, it must meet state or federal requirements for child care homes. The conditions for qualifying for this funding include:

1. The home is able to provide snacks and meals.
2. There is trained staff.
3. Health services are available.
4. Medical records are kept for each child.

23

GATHERING FACTS ON A FAMILY CHILDCARE HOME

1. Name _____
   Phone _____
   Address _____ (cross-streets)
2. Experience of caregiver _____
3. Length of time home has been operating _____
4. Transportation easy? Yes _____ No _____
5. Is the home licensed? Yes _____ No _____
   Did you see the license? Yes _____ No _____
6. Can the caregiver care for a child who becomes ill or has an accident? Yes _____ No _____
7. Is a complete first aid kit available?
   Yes _____ No _____
8. Is there an "emergency form" available giving your permission for care, just in case?
   Yes _____ No _____
9. Does the home keep information on the child and on his/her development? Yes _____ No _____
10. Are parents expected to be part of the program?
    Yes _____ No _____
11. Can you have the names and phone numbers of other parents who use the home? (You should contact some of the other parents to verify they have been satisfied with the service.)
    Yes _____ No _____

12. Can you visit? Yes _____ No _____
    Date of visit _____

13. How many and what are the ages of the children in the home each day?

    _____

14. What is the daily schedule? What kinds of activities available?

    _____

    _____

15. What type of discipline is used? _____

    _____

    How are problems handled? _____

    _____

16. Does the home have safety features (sockets covered, no loose carpets, "child-proof" table tops, child-proof latches on kitchen cabinets)?
    Yes _____ No _____

17. Is the bathroom and outdoors easily and safely accessible? Yes _____ No _____

18. Has the caregiver obtained some training?
    Yes _____ No _____

19. Is there an emergency person available to help out if caregiver becomes ill? Yes _____ No _____

20. Are the equipment, toys, and other supplies in good order and in adequate number for the number of children? Yes _____ No _____

(Review the checklist on childcare centers for additional aspects to look for.)

Overall Impression: Excellent _____ Good _____ Fair _____

24

▲▲

MAKING FAMILY CHILDCARE WORK

The family childcare home has the responsibility to provide the toys, facilities, activities, and supervision necessary for programs that are safe, stimulating, and interesting for a child. Your responsibility is to be sure to deliver and pick up your child on time. Discuss this with the caregiver, but usually you may bring along any items your child may need, such as special food, favorite toys, diapers, a change of clothing, and a toothbrush.

Make sure you give the caregiver any necessary special instructions. Talk with the caregiver about holidays, emergencies, and vacations. If the home is providing before-and after-school care, make sure you report the hours your child is in school and under what special circumstances (if licensing regulations permit) the child can have friends over after school (with previous agreement). Also reach agreements on how and when payment is to be made, whether in cash or by check, and if there are any fees or charges for the time missed, and any other additional responsibilities. Agree on terms for ending the arrangement.

After you have talked over the arrangements and the specific agreements, put them on paper, so that they can be referred to at a later time by both of you to avoid misunderstanding and problems.

Family childcare homes can give children security and stability while providing for each child's individual differences. Many family childcare homes have formed networks with each other to provide services such as counseling, housecleaning, staff-training workshops, and parenting workshops.

Most of the characteristics of good family childcare homes are included in keys on typical programs, qualities to look for in caregivers, and searching for a family childcare home. Some additional points to remember are to have your agreements and arrangements in writing, to be on time to pick up your child unless you have made arrangements ahead of time, and to be thoughtful of the caregiver.

The family childcare home can provide care at moderate cost. It can be convenient to your work or your home. As a nurturing environment for your child while you are at work, it can be an excellent childcare arrangement.

25

〜〜〜〜〜〜〜〜〜〜〜〜〜〜〜〜〜〜〜〜〜〜〜〜〜〜〜〜〜〜〜〜〜

SEARCH FOR A CHILDCARE CENTER

C hildcare centers may be privately run or sponsored by the government, churches, community organizations, employers, unions, or other groups. The programs are usually run by teachers, who have had specialized training in early childhood education.

Your community may have a private or franchised center that is part of a for-profit company in the business of childcare. Many of these programs do meet children's needs and have good facilities. The teachers generally are trained by the company. These programs emphasize a physical environment where the children are safe and are given good care during the day. But the quality of service of franchised centers does vary from place to place. Check to see what is included at your local for-profit center; not all private programs are consistently good. You have to weigh each program separately just as you evaluate any childcare program.

Some employers provide their employees with childcare at the place of employment or at a nearby privately operated program where they pay part or all of the cost. The employees' children are guaranteed a place at these childcare centers. Frequently colleges and universities will have childcare centers, sometimes connected with student unions or the Education Department, operated by the students or faculty. A problem with these programs is that they often are closed during the school holidays and the summer. This may be inconvenient if you are working besides attending school.

Other programs are subsidized by state and federal dollars. They are run by a local government agency and serve low) and middle-income families. Usually the fees are on a sliding scale. Sometimes these programs are underfunded, understaffed, and over-enrolled. You want to be sure this is not the case with the program you choose for your child.

Another kind of program is the drop-in center. Here the charge is by the hour. They may be operated in connection with a shopping center or college. They are convenient for short-term situations.

There are centers that offer special services to handicapped children, where a highly trained staff is available to meet complex needs. Sometimes childcare centers are associated with hospitals and schools.

Since there are many types of childcare centers, a good way to begin your search is to request a list of centers in your area from your state licensing agency (see the list of agencies at the back of this book). The list you receive may include more than just names, addresses, and phone numbers. It may also contain information on things such as age levels, number of children, number of people on staff, and fees, which might help you narrow down the choices.

The next step is to start making telephone calls. With paper and pencil in hand, use the list of questions on pages 42–43 to make your initial contact with the different centers in your area.

Make appointments to visit each center that seems to be a possibility based on what you have learned from the telephone interviews. During your visit you should observe the activities, the way the children are treated, and the general atmosphere of the place. You should be able to talk with the director of each center and get answers to your questions. You will want your child to visit for awhile before you make a final decision.

Your observation of the program is crucial. You want to compare the number of children to the number of adults active in their care. This is called the "child/staff ratio." The number of adults per child can be an important indication of the quality of the program. For example, one caregiver is recommended for every five or six children under the age of three, while there should be one caregiver for every seven to nine children between the ages of three and five.

In addition, you should notice the number of children in small groups within the larger group. It is recommended there be no more than twenty children in a group of three to five-year-olds, and fewer than sixteen to a group if they are under three. For infants, there should not be more than eight children with two adults.

Watch for the amount of attention children get from each adult. See how they are cared for and, when problems come up, how they are handled. Observe the interaction between children. See the quality of the activities, the variety and their appropriateness for the age level of the children. Are activities interesting to the children? Are they easy to understand and yet challenging? Do the children seem happy, at ease, and involved? Does the staff seem to be patient and to enjoy being with children?

The following keys will give you more specific information about what to look for when you visit each center. You will also find useful checklists that will help you keep track of the information you uncover in your search for the best childcare center for your child.

26

SPECIFICS TO LOOK
FOR IN A CHILDCARE
CENTER

When you observe in the center (or home) you will notice many things. This chapter covers the areas you should pay particular attention to. The checklists that follow this chapter enumerate the points to evaluate.

Environment. Notice whether the surroundings are safe. Are the children free to move around? There should be a good balance between the indoor and outdoor spaces. Quiet areas should allow a place for children to be private. The overall environment should be appropriate for their age, stimulating to them and helpful for learning. It should be clean, bright, and cheerful.

Nutrition. The menus should be nutritionally well-balanced and varied. Notice whether there are a variety of tasty snacks available, such as peanuts, crackers, raisins, carrots, celery, and apple juice. You will want to notice the amount of sugary treats offered. It is highly recommended the amount of sugar given a child be limited. In a good program the children enjoy mealtime. The meals should be served in a comfortable, relaxed family style. Children need to be encouraged to feed themselves and to have enjoyable talk at mealtime. The portions should be the right size for them. They should be encouraged to try new foods. The home or center can expand your child's tastes beyond what you can do at home because children respond to other children's interests in food.

Toilet Training. It is preferable that the child be toilet trained before she or he enters a program. If it is a center caring for infants, see if there are special safe places for diapering. The older child should have easy access to a bathroom whenever he needs one. The facilities should be clean and should have soap and towels.

Health. Ask the director about the type of services available and whether there is a pediatrician and a dentist on call. The children should have a place to store toothbrushes; they should have personal, non-breakable cups or clean paper cups; and time should be set aside for them to brush their teeth.

You will need to provide the staff with an emergency release form. Also, instruct the caregiver if your child has any health problems or is not feeling well.

Rest. Children need a regular rest time and a place where they can sleep or be quiet on a cot or pad.

Toys. Some programs allow the children to bring a favorite toy. Observe what is available. If you wish, ask the director about bringing a toy from home. You may also want to donate some toys to the program. Toys should be safe, clean, appropriate, kept in good repair, and easily accessible to the children. If battery-operated toys are included in the program, they should be in good working condition.

Illness. Usually, children are not allowed to come to the center if they have a communicable disease. However, if the child becomes ill during the day, there should be a quiet place where the child can rest and be taken care of. If the center agrees to care for a child who is ill, be sure to give instructions to the director on special needs and dispensing medications during the day.

Education. Make sure all your questions about the educational services of the program are answered. Any questions your child may have should be answered also. How the staff responds is an important indication of the overall quality of the program. Children should be able to make decisions and discuss their needs with the staff and the director. You will want to notice whether the children have opportunities to talk among themselves, to share and discuss ideas, and whether they feel free to express themselves. You will want to know what kind of schedule the educational program follows each day. You can follow up at home by reading, talking, and practicing the new skills with your child.

Acknowledgment and Attention. The way in which the children are greeted on arriving is important. You will want to know how and by whom this is done each day. It is important to say hello and goodbye to children as they come and go each day. You will want to notice whether the small groups of children are happy, active, and involved. If the atmosphere in the program is informal and the children seem to be treated with consideration and respect, you will have a good indication the program is of good quality.

Atmosphere. You will know you are in a good program if children feel free and comfortable with each other and the adults. If children appear to have their problems resolved with a minimum of physical aggressiveness, if children seem to work and play well together, and if the attitude appears to be one of cooperation and enjoyment, you can feel confident about the program. Discipline should be fair and not abusive. Special occasions, such as birthdays, should be observed. You should be able to arrange for cake and ice cream in advance with the director.

Activities. Look for a balance between work and play. Time should be allowed for cleaning up and for toys to be put away. You want to be sure the children have a variety of interesting activities to engage in, that there is freedom to talk, move and interact with each other, as well as time for snacks and play outdoors, and that trips are arranged to places in the neighboring area. Notice the kinds and number of toys, equipment, and furniture, how the toys are stored, whether they are sturdy and of good quality, and whether they can be reached easily.

If there is outdoor play, there should be safe and sturdy climbing materials, and equipment that can take hard wear. Sand, dirt, and water play should be available. For adequate play and active movement approximately seventy-five square feet per child is usually recommended for outside play areas for centers; indoors thirty-five square feet is considered adequate. If a park is nearby, the outdoor area may be small and the park used as a substitute. The physical space should be clear of obstructions. Basic standards of cleanliness and safety should be met. Inside fabrics should be fire-resistant. Indoor and outdoor first-aid equipment should be complete and easily accessible. The area should be free from dangerous objects and substances both in- and outdoors. The entire facility should be painted with cheerful, colorful, lead-free paint. Ask about safety features if you have any doubts. Check to see that the indoor temperature is comfortable, and there is adequate light and ventilation.

The checklists that follow will serve as a concise guide of what to look for when you visit. Each place will be different, although you may find certain similarities.

You will want to visit as many places as you can. Visit at least three programs before making a final decision. Use the checklists each time. Record your answers for each center on a separate piece of paper, so that you will have a record of your impressions to review later.

Look at the whole place, inside and out. Is the center inviting and a nice place to be? Words like homey, comfortable or cold, and cluttered might occur to you. Is the place physically well-arranged and attractive, or is it crowded and impersonal? You will get a sense of these things as you walk around and observe.

You may feel uncomfortable about taking the checklists into the center you are visiting. But you should also feel confident that you are well-equipped to make the best selection possible. The director and staff should be respectful of your actions and concerns. If you prefer, you can become thoroughly familiar with what the checklists cover and leave them in your purse, if you wish, and then fill them out right after you complete each visit.

Caregivers should welcome the parents' concerns and interest. An informed parent is an asset to any childcare situation. But if the caregiver appears to feel uncomfortable being judged in this way, try to be sensitive to this feeling while you gather your information as unobtrusively as possible. You should take as much time as you need for this process. Two hours is a good amount of time to learn about a childcare center—to talk with the director, with the teachers, and see the children move through several different activities. If you are not certain after reviewing the checklists and thinking about your feelings about the center, pay another visit, or talk with other parents about their experiences. Try to attend a parent-teacher meeting. Good communication between the staff and parents is one of the important ways to determine the quality of the program and helps to make the childcare situation successful for everyone.

27

~~~~~~

GATHERING FACTS ON A CHILDCARE CENTER

1. Name of the Director _____
   Phone_____
2. Name and address of center (cross streets)

   _____
   _____
   Experience of caregiver _____
3. Transportation easy? Yes _____ No _____
4. Does the center have a license?
   Yes _____ No _____
   Did you see the license? Yes _____ No _____
5. Length of time center has been operating ____
   _____
6. Is there a first-aid kit? Yes _____ No _____
   Is emergency care available when the child becomes ill? Yes _____ No _____
7. Does the center keep information/records on
   the children and their development?
   Yes _____ No _____
8. Are parents expected to be part of the center?
   Yes _____ No _____
9. Will the director provide you with the names of
   other parents who use the center?
   Yes _____ No _____
10. What are the center's hours? _____
11. What does it cost? _____
    Affordable? Yes _____ No _____

12. Can you visit? Yes _____ No _____
    Date of visit _____

Overall impression: Excellent _____ Good _____
Fair _____ Poor _____
Comments: _____
_____
_____
_____

28

PHYSICAL FACILITY CHECKLIST

The physical space in which a child spends time is important. Environment is crucial to growth and development. The space allocated should be at least thirty-five square feet for every child enrolled. While you will want to check out safety and creative use of the play areas and equipment, keep in mind that an older place lacking the latest or fanciest equipment may have other features that make it more than adequate.

1. Does the space seem safe? (Adequate lighting and electric sockets covered, out of reach, and safety type?) Yes _____ No _____

2. Is there enough space, well planned, and without crowding? Yes _____ No _____

3. Is the equipment inside and out varied, sturdy, safe, and easy for a child to use?
Yes _____ No _____

4. Is the place attractive and comfortable? (Are there plants, pets, and special activity areas?)
Yes _____ No _____

5. Can the children get inside and outside safely and without difficulty? Yes _____ No _____

6. Are the materials ample, in good condition, and easily available? (Can children reach a variety of books, toys, art supplies, etc?)
Yes _____ No _____

7. Are the bathroom facilities clean and easy for a child to use? (Easy-to-reach faucets, toilets, toothbrushes and toothpaste, soap, paper towels, etc.?) Yes _____ No _____

8. Are the meals nutritious and well balanced, and is the food prepared and served attractively? Yes _____ No _____

9. Do the children have a comfortable and quiet place for naps? Are there individual beds, cots, or mats to sleep on? Yes _____ No _____

10. Do the children have a place to keep their own belongings? (A place or storage for a change of clothes?) Yes _____ No _____

11. Does the place have provisions for an ill child? A first-aid kit? Staff who can assist in emergencies? A quiet place to rest? Yes _____ No _____

FINAL TALLY OF PHYSICAL FACILITIES

Total number of Yes answers _____

Total number of No answers _____

Words I would use to describe the place _____

_____

Would my child feel comfortable in this place? _____

_____

Do I feel comfortable in this place? _____

_____

The physical space should be clean, well-equipped, comfortable, and safe. How the place looks is important, as it tells you a great deal about the quality of a program and the people involved in it. You will learn more about what to look for as you compare different programs and notice both obvious and subtle differences. Be sure your choice meets the basic health standards of safety, adequate play and learning areas and a warm, comfortable environment for the child.

29

~~~~~~

EMOTIONAL CLIMATE CHECKLIST

What happens emotionally to the children in the environment is most critical. A place that needs paint can still be a place of love and attention. Beyond the basic care they need, children are affected by the way staff interact with them and with the other children. Among other important concerns, you need to know how discipline is handled and how comfortable the children are with each other.

1. Do the children show they really like and trust the adults? Yes _____ No _____

2. Do the children appear happy, comfortable, and relaxed? Yes _____ No _____

3. Does the staff communicate easily with each child? Do they communicate well with each other? Yes _____ No _____

4. Does the discipline reflect my philosophy? Yes _____ No _____

5. Are the children allowed to pursue their own interests according to their abilities? Yes _____ No _____

6. Are the children's emotional needs given first priority? Yes _____ No _____

7. Would my child receive the attention he needs and be treated fairly here? Yes _____ No _____

8. Are problems handled without upset?
   Yes _____ No _____
9. Does the director or teacher answer my questions openly? Yes _____ No _____
10. Do I feel comfortable with the staff and the place? Yes _____ No _____

FINAL TALLY OF EMOTIONAL CLIMATE
Total number of Yes answers _____
Total number of No answers _____

Words I would use to describe the emotional climate

_____

How would my child feel about this place? _____

_____

How do I feel about this place? _____

_____

Some of the emotional aspects listed may be hard to spot as they are not as obvious as the toys or learning materials available. Therefore, you need to spend time in each place you are considering to get a sense of the way the adults relate to each other and to the children. You may get additional information by talking with other parents whose children have been involved in the program for some time. How the child is treated is the most important part of the whole program. You should notice the way children respond to each other and to the adults as indicators that they are comfortable, feel cared about, respected, and treated fairly.

30

^^

LEARNING CHECKLIST

An important part of any childcare program is the number and quality of learning opportunities offered. Trips and extra activities add richness to the overall program. Childcare can prepare your child for the lifelong enjoyment of learning, both in formal schooling and outside of school.

Parents should be able to follow their child's learning progress in the center or home. The staff should keep the parents informed about the child's progress. Parents also learn from the child's experiences, from the teachers, and from each other.

1. Is the place arranged for easy learning with a good selection and supply of appropriate educational materials and toys? Are the materials used by the children? Yes _____ No _____

2. Does the program seem well planned? Yes _____ No _____

3. Does the program provide many different opportunities for the individual child? Yes _____ No _____

4. Can children move around and find appropriate materials easily? Is storage of materials adequate? Yes _____ No _____

5. Are the learning activities understood by the children? Yes _____ No _____

6. Are the children's questions answered by the staff promptly and completely?
Yes _____ No _____

7. Do the children enjoy the activities?
Yes _____ No _____

8. Do the children receive enough individual attention and assistance? Yes _____ No _____

9. Are special events and local field trips arranged frequently? Yes _____ No _____

10. Do the children have opportunities to express themselves through drawing and craft projects, and are these displayed for them and available for the parents to take home?
Yes _____ No _____

FINAL TALLY ON LEARNING ENVIRONMENT

Total number of Yes answers _____
Total number of No answers _____

What is taught and how is it taught? _____

_____

Words I would use to describe the educational opportunities. _____

_____ _____

How do I feel about the learning opportunities here?

_____

Certainly the program provides many formal and informal learning opportunities. The training and experience of the staff is an indication of their qualifications for teaching young children in ways they can understand and get the most value from. Children in the early years learn rapidly and need the right information, materials, and techniques to help them gain the most from the learning experiences offered.

90

31

~~~~~~

SOCIAL CHECKLIST

The opportunity the center or home provides for the children to get to know each other and contribute something special to each other is a vital part of the program. When staff relate to the children in a warm and supportive way, children respond happily. They learn easily and play with each other contentedly. Children need attention, support, and understanding whether their personalities are aggressive, outgoing, or shy.

1. Do I like how the children behave and relate to each other? Yes _____ No _____
2. Are conflicts handled with sensitivity? Yes _____ No _____
3. Would my child fit in with the group? Yes _____ No _____
4. Would my child make friends here? Yes _____ No _____
5. Are the language and culture of each child respected? Yes _____ No _____
6. Do the children respond easily and happily to each other? Yes _____ No _____
7. Do the children have many conflicts? Are they given help if needed? Yes _____ No _____
8. Are the children encouraged to settle arguments without adult intervention? Yes _____ No _____
9. Does the staff encourage children to express themselves and participate? Yes _____ No _____

10. Are the children learning nonsexist social roles?
    Yes _____ No _____
11. Are the parents made to feel welcome and encouraged to know each other?
    Yes _____ No _____

FINAL TALLY ON SOCIAL CHECKLIST
Total number of Yes answers _____
Total number of No answers _____

Words I would use to describe the social experiences (advantages and disadvantages) _____
_____

How would I feel about being a parent in this place?
_____

How would my child feel in this place? _____
_____

The child changes rapidly during these early years and learns a great deal from observing, playing, and interacting with other children. It is essential that the staff help the children when necessary, but not interfere with their interactions. You will notice a lot about the way children relate to each other when you observe the program. Picture your child in the middle of the group of children and imagine how he or she will relate to the other children. You should be made welcome and be allowed to visit not only at the time you are making your decision, but later, when you can visit and help out. If you feel comfortable while you are visiting and see that your child fits in also, you have found the right place.

32

THE MOST IMPORTANT POINTS

This overview of the most important aspects will assist you in getting a complete picture of the program. The most important points include practical considerations such as cost, the physical facility, safety and comfort; emotional points, such as how the children are treated; and learning aspects such as the quality of activities offered. Ideally, everything will be in place and fit all your needs, but a program with a perfect score is hard to find. Be careful, selective, and insistent on obtaining the answers to the questions you need most to know. Then make the final decision based on your feelings, observations, and information you gather.

1. I can afford the fees at this place.
   Yes _____ No _____
2. The place can be reached easily.
   Yes _____ No _____
3. The place is safe, comfortable, and attractive.
   Yes _____ No _____
4. The place has plenty of good and varied toys and equipment for fun and learning.
   Yes _____ No _____
5. Children and staff interact happily and communicate easily. Yes _____ No _____
6. The place offers nutritious, tasty meals and snacks. Yes _____ No _____
7. Each child is respected as an individual.
   Yes _____ No _____

8. Each child has the opportunity and space for a wide range of activities, either for playing with other children or for playing quietly by himself or herself. Yes _____ No _____

9. My needs for the caregiver to be dependable and value me as a parent are considered. Yes _____ No _____

10. The place is suitable for my child and my situation. Yes _____ No _____

RATING

Each Yes answer = 5 points

Total number of items = 10

Total number of Yes answers _____ × 5 = _____

Total points for Yes answers _____

40–50 Excellent program. Seriously consider it.

30–40 Good program. Think some more.

20–30 Fair program. Don't use it if you can avoid it.

Fewer than 20. Definitely continue your search.

A final comment on the checklist: If in each area—physical, emotional, learning, and social—you have more Yes than No answers, you have found a place that probably will care for your child well. If not, do not be discouraged. Continue your search until you find the most appropriate place for your child and one that will meet your standards for quality.

33

∧∧∧

SEARCH FOR AN
IN-HOME CAREGIVER

To find a person who is kind, gentle, and knows how and when to respond to your child in a positive and interested way is not easy. People who are well qualified for this work are in high demand and earn high salaries. Sometimes, on a part-time basis, you may be able to obtain the services of an elderly person, a retired teacher, a part-time student, or a relative. Or you may join with one or two other parents to hire someone who would care for all the children in one of your homes. This is called *shared-care*.

Before you begin your search for an in-home caregiver, think about what you expect of the person you hire. Will you want the caregiver's sole responsibility to be caring for your child, or will you also want her to do light housekeeping, cooking, laundry, or chauffeuring? Would you prefer to have someone live in, out, or in during the week and out on weekends? How many hours per day do you need the caregiver? What are those hours? How many days and which days? Do you need someone for evenings as well? How important is it to you to have a caregiver who can be very flexible about her hours to accommodate frequent changes in your own schedule? Make a job description list of these items and refer to it when you make your telephone calls.

There are several avenues to take in your search for an in-home caregiver. Explore all of them simultaneously to increase your chances of finding a qualified person.

Call or write to your state licensing agency and any community referral agencies in your area. The state licensing agency and your community referral agencies will probably give you names of local, private agencies rather than the names of individuals to contact. Then you will have to follow up by calling the private agencies. You should also look in the Yellow Pages for telephone numbers of private nanny agencies in your area.

The private agencies try to match up your needs with prospective caregivers, which can save you a lot of time. Be aware, though, that the placement fees these agencies charge can run anywhere from $300 to $2000.

Tell everyone you know that you are looking for an in-home caregiver. Speak to people like your pediatrician, associates at work, and parents of your children's friends, as well as relatives, friends, and neighbors. Contact local schools, colleges, churches, and community groups. Put up notices at the laundromat, supermarket, community center, university, or any location where people may come who you feel would be competent to care for your child. Also, check bulletin boards in these places for advertisements posted by potential caregivers.

Place an appropriate ad in your local newsapers. The ad should include:

1. Family description (single, married, number of people).
2. Live in or out.
3. General location of your home.
4. Age and sex of children.
5. Brief job descriptions (light housekeeping, cooking, laundry, chauffeuring).
6. Days of week and hours needed.

7. Special requirements, such as nonsmoker, driver with own car.
8. Phone number and when to call.

Do not include your name, address, or salary stipulations in the ad.

Look at the Situation Wanted ads in area newspapers. Call to get more information about anything that sounds promising.

Once you have names of individuals or agencies to contact, it is time to start making telephone calls. The questions you should ask are discussed in the next Key, Interviewing an In-Home Caregiver.

34

^^

INTERVIEWING AN IN-HOME CAREGIVER

To weed out people who do not have the qualifications you are looking for, talk to each person over the phone for at least five to ten minutes. This should be a quiet, uninterrupted time, so you and the caller can relax and talk easily. If either of you is hurried, ask the person to call back and set a time for the return call.

During the call you should:

1. Explain your situation briefly.
2. Find out about the person's background and experience:
   Does she have any training in early childhood education or child development?
   What age children has she cared for?
   What sex?
   How many?
   How long has she been doing this?
   Why did she leave her last position?
3. Write down the names and phone numbers of references, names of previous employers, length of time worked, and duties.
4. Get a sense of what this person is like, whether you feel good about her, and what she has to offer.

If you think the person is a good possibility, ask the following questions:

1. Do you want a regular situation now?
2. For how long would you be interested in working?
3. What makes you interested in this position?
4. How do you think children should be disciplined? (Allow them time to explain how they would handle your child in different situations.)
5. What are your thoughts about preparing food or feeding children?
6. What are your thoughts about toilet habits?
7. Do you have any health problems that will affect your work?
8. Have you had a medical checkup and chest X-ray recently?
9. Do you drink? Smoke?
10. Have you ever been charged with a crime?
11. Do you drive?
12. How would you get here?
13. Describe some of the different activities you would do with children.
14. How do you feel about children watching television?
15. What do you charge? What benefits do you require?
16. What hours are you available?
17. When can you begin?

When you are interviewing a mature teenager or college student for an after-school caregiver job, ask if they have had experience caring for younger brothers and sisters or other children.

After you have reviewed the important points over the phone and are satisfied that the person is a real prospect, then arrange for your potential caregiver to come to your house. Show your prospective caregiver around the house. Describe the things you want her to do and explain what your child is like. You may prefer to have everything written down so as not to forget any important details.

During this interview, again review the previous questions and be sure you have the answers to your questions. Introduce the person to your child or children and note their reactions. It is important that they relate well to each other. See whether the person seems flexible, has a warm and affectionate nature, and responds and talks easily to your child. If she moves in too quickly on the child or gushes or is overly sweet and solicitous, the child may withdraw or feel intimidated. It is better if the child comes to her.

Be sure to check references, and talk to two or three of the people for whom the person has worked. Ask them how long they have known the person, in what capacity she worked for them, what her responsibilities were, whether they found her to be a dependable employee, whether she was reliable in arriving at their home on time, what her strong and weak points are, why she left. If the person worked as a caregiver for the reference you are calling, ask how she acts with children, whether the children liked her, how she got along with the children, how she treated them. Finally, ask whether they would hire the person again.

In addition to checking the person's references, check with your local police to see whether she has a record as a child abuser or sex offender.

35

‸‸‸

HIRING AN IN-HOME CAREGIVER

You should spell out exactly the terms of employment for the person you hire. This will include:

1. the hours of work
2. salary
3. Social Security and income tax deductions
4. sick leave
5. vacations
6. insurance
7. when salary will be paid
8. whether salary will be paid in cash or by check
9. additional duties expected, such as housekeeping, shopping or meal preparation
10. payment for overtime or additional duties
11. rules regarding drinking, smoking, television watching, visitors, and telephone use
12. giving notice

In addition to discussing the details with the caregiver, give her a written copy of the "agreement" and keep a copy for yourself. Be sure to explain to the caregiver what your child is like, how your home operates, what he or she can expect in terms of snacks and food, any special problems with the house, off-limits areas, and so forth. If you do not want the caregiver to have people over when you are away

101

or use your telephone for personal calls, be sure to say so right away.

Be sure to put in writing anything that is necessary for emergencies, including a medical release form. Put the form and other written instructions and phone numbers in a permanent place next to the telephone. The instructions should include numbers where you can be reached and the number of a close relative or friend the caregiver can get in touch with during the day if you are not easily available. Also list numbers for the doctor, fire department, police, ambulance, and poison control center.

To be effective the caregiver will need as much information from you as possible about your child. List the child's routines, special toys and equipment, specific habits, needs or problems, and anything else you can think of that will help her understand your child. Do not be concerned about sharing this information. The caregiver does not take over your role as parent, but helps play a part in your child's life, and helps you, too.

Check the house to see whether there are any potential hazards the caregiver should know about. Make sure the caregiver knows how to apply first aid and where the first-aid kit is. You may want to put together a special childcare kit, containing pencils and crayons, paper, yarn, envelopes, toys, tissues, flashlight, adhesive bandages, antiseptic, activity books, and child-related magazines.

The relationship between the caregiver and the parent should be honest and open. You want the caregiver to feel free to talk to you about the child's behavior while you are gone and to give you any additional information you need to know. Also make time to get to know the caregiver on a personal basis—ask questions about the person's family, life experience, and interests. This person can be a real friend to you beyond the job itself. Your mutual relationship is important for the child's security and well-being. Make a regular time to talk over your child's activities while you are gone. Show your appreciation to the caregiver in the form of acknowledgements for her work, paid bonuses, and an occasional thoughtful gift. When you treat your caregiver well it will not only improve your own relationship but that of the caregiver and your child.

36

MAKING YOUR
DECISION

By now you have visited a number of centers and homes and interviewed several caregivers. Before you make your final selection, review your experiences and think about what you are going to do next.

Take some time, sit down, and really think about all the things you have seen and heard. Separate the real possibilities from all the options. If you are still confused or uncertain about what you want and need for your child and yourself, it's understandable. You will seldom find a perfect arrangement, even when the place looks perfect on the surface, but certainly it can be close.

By this time, however, you will be pretty certain about what type of care will suit your child best—home, center, caregiver, or alternative. You will probably choose the type of arrangement that most appeals to you and that you can afford. The discussion on planning your budget will assist you in reaching this decision.

In going through the checklists, match up the goals and needs of you and your child (as you defined them earlier) with what each situation has to offer. You might want to do this with a friend or adviser so you can be sure to consider all your options.

Finally, you have seen a variety of places, talked to a lot of people, and are attempting to make the right decision.

These questions will help you make your selection process easier. Ask yourself:

1. Which place feels best to you?
2. Did you like the way the place looked?
3. Were appropriate things provided for the children?
4. Did you like the way the staff knew each child and talked to each one?
5. How would your child fit in?
6. Is there anything further you want to know about the program? If you have any doubts or want more information, contact a few of the parents to talk over your concerns and get answers to your questions.
7. Is the place convenient and accessible by car or public transportation?
8. Is the place near your workplace?
9. Will your child receive good emergency care if an accident occurs or an illness arises?
10. Will the hours of the place coincide with your work schedule?
11. Will parent meetings and other commitments fit your time schedule?
12. Are these meetings arranged at convenient times with consideration for parents and children?
13. If you cannot attend evening meetings, are there other ways you can be involved in the program?
14. Are the other parents you have spoken with happy with the place, the staff, and the way their own children are making progress? If not, find out why. Talking with other parents is very important for you and for the children.
15. Will you be allowed to be with your child the

first days, until you and your child feel comfortable with the arrangement and adjust?
16. Can you visit when you want to?

If the answer to all of these questions is positive, and the fee fits your budget, this could be your best choice. If you have additional questions and are not certain, continue looking. This careful selection will pay off over time. This is why the search for childcare often takes several weeks.

You might want to develop a secondary plan for childcare for the future and put your name on the waiting list if your first choice has no openings. Maybe you can find space there later or a better arrangement in just six months or a year. What's your second choice if this situation doesn't work out? Often, as time goes on, you become more familiar with childcare opportunities in your area, and selecting childcare becomes easier. Contact the local resource and referral service regularly to learn about new programs.

37

wwwwwwwwwwwwwwwwwwwwwwwwwwwwwwwwwwwwwwwwwwwwwwwwwwww

INFORMATION YOU NEED TO PREPARE AHEAD

B efore you leave your child at a center, home, or with a caregiver, you will need to provide the staff with the following information.

1. Your name
2. Your address
3. Your phone number (at home)
4. Your child's name
5. The birth date, height, and weight of your child
6. Phone numbers where the parents can be reached during the day
7. Work schedule
8. Emergency numbers of a friend or relative, and doctor and/or dentist. Also provide a signed release for emergency care.
9. Medical information, dates of immunizations, any allergies, last physical examination
10. Special needs or problems, medications
11. Information on development (ages your child walked, talked and was toilet-trained)
12. Health habits, eating, sleeping, etc.
13. Information on brothers and sisters, ages and special considerations

14. Income and related financial information if you are applying for scholarship aid
15. Transportation arrangements

Most centers require the child to have a recent physical examination and have all necessary immunizations.

If the program you are considering requires you to sign a contract these items will be in the agreement:

1. Fees you will pay (cash or check; fees for overtime)
2. Due dates of payments
3. Days your child will come to the center
4. Hours your child will be there
5. How you will transport the child to and from the center
6. A list of services the caregiver will provide (this includes meals, snacks, indoor and outdoor activities, toys, games and play equipment)
7. A list of your responsibilities (this includes arrival and pick up as expected, providing personal items, instructions for medicine or special diets)
8. Trip release agreement and extra funds to cover outings if needed

The contract should also cover anything else that is important. Before you sign the document, ask any questions that occur to you. Bring a copy of the contract home to keep in your files.

Keep the contract handy. It may specify what items the director expects parents to bring for the children, such as changes of clothing, special toys, and educational materials.

38

PREPARING YOUR CHILD FOR CHILDCARE

E very member of the family, including the children, is affected by a mother's return to work. You can prepare the children for separation by simple overnights at other friends' homes, or by leaving them with other people, such as relatives, caregivers, and friends, for short periods of time. You will come to learn that other adults can care for your children, and the children will learn that you come back for them. Childcare does not change your primary relationship with your child.

By the age of four, a child should be able to care for himself to a certain extent. For example, he should be able to brush his teeth, comb his hair, dress and undress, put on his shoes, go to the bathroom, and wash his hands. Teaching these self-help skills is one of the responsibilities of parents. Children are learning informally to tell time, and match colors, sizes and shapes. Talk to your children about books and ideas, take trips with them to nearby places, answer their questions, and also make sure they can understand and follow directions. These are all good ways to prepare them to enjoy and get the most out of their time away from you.

If you are returning to work, you will want to encourage your child to learn other skills, such as putting away his toys, setting the table, using a fork and knife, and pouring from a container. As children learn these self-help skills, they get a sense of accomplishment and heightened self-esteem.

109

The older child should be able to take responsibility for keeping his own room straight, and can help with dusting, watering plants, tending the garden, and feeding pets. When mother goes to work, she cannot also handle all of the responsibilities of the home. The more the family works cooperatively together, the better it is for everyone.

Sharing some of your thoughts and plans with your child the week prior to the change is important. As you are getting dressed, you can say, "Soon I will be going to work, and you'll be going to a new school where you can have a good time with some other children. We will have to get dressed and have breakfast earlier in the morning to get to the center. You'll have a chance to play with the other children. I think you'll like it very much." Another example of how you might talk with your child about the new childcare arrangement would be:

> "Susie, Mommy will be going back to work and you are going to have time to play with other children at a special place. Mrs. Smith is a person who enjoys taking care of children. We have talked about having you stay with her while Mommy is at work. I'm sure you will like her very much and will enjoy being with other children. We will be going to Mrs. Smith's in a couple of days and I wanted you to know about it. We will visit the office tomorrow so you will know where Mommy is going to work. Mrs. Smith will always be able to reach me there by telephone so you can talk to me any time you need to. I will take you there each morning, and when I finish work I will pick you up in the afternoon."

When the time for separation comes, be direct and reassuring with your child. You are going away and you will return. This can be done without deception, games or emotional trauma.

Your child will know by your tone of voice and your attitude what to expect from this new situation, so it is important to have a positive attitude when you talk about it. Under no circumstances should you leave your child without telling him what will be happening to him. If the child is well prepared, the experience has a better chance of becoming a happy one.

Children can cope with new experiences if they are prepared physically and emotionally. A simple rule is: the better your child is prepared, the more he will benefit from the experience.

39

‸‸‸

FIRST DAYS AND WEEKS

You have checked out all the possible arrangements and have finally selected a program. Now your child needs your support and understanding during these first days.

Before the first day, ask the staff about their policy on personal objects from home and how they want you to handle clothing, food, toys, and other personal items. If toys from home are allowed, ask your child if he or she wants to bring a toy or another familiar item.

The child's clothing should be wash-and-wear, easy to put on and take off, and made to take the rough and tumble play with other children. Be sure to label each article of clothing with the child's name to make sure it does not get lost. Pack an extra pair of play pants and underwear in a bag marked with your child's name. Also provide an extra toothbrush, cup and toothpaste, washcloth and towel.

Make sure the staff has your phone number at work and an emergency number of a friend or relative to call if for any reason you cannot be reached. Complete information should be left with the staff before you leave your child. If you have made a sincere effort to investigate the childcare situation thoroughly, when you leave your child for the first time, you will be able to do so with peace of mind. You should be able to work or do whatever you have planned in full confidence. If you are relaxed and comfortable, your child will be too.

Prepare your child for the first day by talking about being at a nice new place where he or she will meet and play with other children. Mention you will leave him there while you go to work. Remind him that the person there will know where you are all the time and can call you if necessary.

It is up to the center director or the family childcare home caregiver to give you permission to stay with your child the first day or as long as necessary. Ask if you may bring your lunch and eat with your child the first day. Be there, but let your child find his or her own way. When the children are engaged in an activity, you may be able to assist. If for some reason you will not be able to stay for the entire day, tell your child earlier that you will be leaving and will be back later to take him or her home. If you think your child will be upset by this, arrange your schedule so you will not have to leave, or if you must leave, return as soon as possible. You may also want to leave for a few hours just to allow your child a chance to be there without you. You could ask the director or a member of the staff to find a child to take your child under his or her wing. Having a friend makes the child's adjustment easier. The important thing is to make this change as smooth as possible. The staff will probably give you a lot of friendly assistance, so include them in your plans.

You can say as you are getting ready to go the first morning, "I'm going to take you to Mrs. Jones's house. You can play with the other children while I talk to her. Then I'll be leaving." Or you can say, "I'm going to take you there and stay with you awhile. Then I'll be going to work."

Stay at the center or home at least until the teacher or caregiver talks directly to your child and your child wishes to begin an activity. Sometimes this first conversation involves asking your child's name and making a name tag, or inviting your child to begin a game or join a circle of children engaged in a song or story. The important thing is to be there, with the teacher's permission, long enough for your child to feel comfortable before the two of you part. You might want to go out of the room for a while to see how your child does without you. Some children will move right into the group and begin to participate immediately and comfortably from the first hour. Others will benefit from their parents' sensitive watching and sharing until the strangeness and newness wears off a bit. For some it may take a day, for others a week, and for others still longer. Do not push or rush your child. Being sensitive to your child's responses at the outset will save a lot of unnecessary aggravation later.

Your child is unique and like no other at the center or home. Make sure the staff knows your child as well as possible before you leave and that they recognize some of the subtle needs your child has expressed to you. These needs and your own should always be respected and given attention.

Although it is best for your child's emotional well-being to make the transition to the new place gradually, this is often impossible. You may not be able to get time off from work. Or the caregiver you have chosen might prefer to introduce your child to other children without you there. In each case, tell your child ahead of time a little about what to expect and what to do. If you have fears, try not to show them. Let your child know you recognize how he or she feels, and guide your child towards coping with the situation alone. No matter what your child can understand intellectually, he or she will respond to what you are saying and pick up cues about how to behave. If you tell children what to expect and what they hear is positive and without fear, the transition can be simple.

40

~~~~~~

BRIDGING THE GAP BETWEEN HOME AND CHILDCARE

In a child's life, a gap opens between the world at home and the world of childcare. A place away from home is not home: it is a new place to learn and grow. Your child should be encouraged to enjoy this place, the new friends, and the fresh experiences. He or she also has a responsibility to participate and make the most of the experience. Remember, do not pressure your child. Just reassure him or her that the new experiences will be a new adventure, valuable to both of you.

During the first few weeks adjust your schedule to make more time to be at the center or home. Let the staff know you are willing to do so as an interested and concerned parent.

Contact the other parents who live nearby to arrange car pools, informal meetings, or sitting swaps. Find out what kind of activities parents are involved in, when the meetings are, and either join what is going on already or simply contribute whatever interests and ideas you have.

Take time each day to talk with the staff about any concerns or information they might need about your child. Tell them about a cold, an upset in the family, a new job, or anything else that in any way would affect your child or interfere with the day's program. You also want the staff to know you are interested in learning about your child's progress, the activities during the day, and any new friends made.

Find out whether there are activities or discussion you can undertake at home to continue the daytime activities. Focus on what happened during the day. Sometimes staff people are eager to tell you only good things about your child. Make it clear to them you are interested in how your child feels, and you accept his or her feelings, good or bad.

Here are some suggestions for things to talk about with the staff at the end of the day:

1. What pleased my child most? What displeased my child?
2. Did my child take a nap?
3. Did my child enjoy the food? What did my child eat?
4. Is there a new food we can talk about and also have at home?
5. Did my child learn a new skill he or she may be able to share?
6. Was there a special activity that could be talked about?
7. Is there a new friend to invite over to play on the weekend?
8. How are my child's relationships with other children and adults?
9. Is there anything I can do to assist?

With the answers to these questions, you can keep in touch with your child's life away from you. If a problem arises, you'll have an idea where it started and be able to respond more effectively.

The staff also needs to know what is happening with your child at home. Your child may arrive with particular needs that day.

Here are some things to tell the staff at the beginning of the day:

1. What's going on at home of concern to your child
2. Any physical or emotional problems
3. A new experience your child has had
4. What your child tells you regarding the program
5. What changes you see in your child related to the program such as new abilities, interests, and attitudes.

Make sure to thank the caregivers for the efforts they make on behalf of your child. They very much appreciate it. Birthdays and other special days, such as Christmas or Channukah, are enhanced by small gifts.

Help your child make the transition from childcare to home by talking about the things that have happened and the things he or she has done during the day. Listening to your child and your caregivers is your way of positively connecting their day with your own.

Do not burden your child or caregivers with complaints about your tough day at the office. It is understandable you will be tired by the end of the day, and that makes it all the more important to take some time for yourself. Understand the responsibilities and work the caregiver had all day.

Some good relaxing activities are taking a walk, or finding a quiet space to breathe deeply and relax. Make sure you have someone to whom you can talk about any concerns or negative feelings.

The time you spend away from your child every day is the time for you to handle your responsibilities in the world. If you can handle each part of your life in a positive way, you will make life easier for yourself and all those involved with you.

41

KNOWING YOUR CHILD IS HAPPY

You know your child best. You can judge with your own eyes and ears what is happening with your child as the time passes. Children usually tell the truth. If your child looks forward to going to the place each day, speaks openly about what happened during the day, brings things home that he or she drew, painted, or made, is able to sleep and eat as usual, and seems generally secure and happy, you know you have made a good choice.

Do not panic at the first problem. There are bound to be some in the first days. Children vary greatly in what they can adapt to and handle. If you share some of the problems with the staff or other parents, solutions usually can be found. Feel free to drop in unannounced to discuss anything or visit for awhile. If for any reason you see that the situation is not working out for you and your child after a few weeks, let the caregiver know about the problems you are having, and start looking for an alternative. Out of consideration, you should not leave without notifying the staff, no matter how discontented you may be.

If any serious problems arise with the caregiver doing anything inappropriate around or to the children, you may want to notify the department of childcare licensing in your area to inform them of a need for a visit by an inspector. Before you do this, however, do talk with other parents to determine if they have had any similar experiences. Serious problems usually can be avoided if you observe your child's behavior, talk with your child, and keep in contact with other parents.

Some of the problems that may arise, such as aggressive behavior on the part of your child or one of the other children, can often be solved by communication. Make appointments with the caregiver so you can discuss your child's progress as well as any other important issues and personal needs. Be calm and understanding when you talk with the director or teachers about problems. It often helps to make a list of what you want to discuss and take it with you to your meeting.

If there are disagreements about the way children are to be disciplined or handled when problems occur, they can be worked out by being clear, direct, and tactful. Talk with other parents to see if they are experiencing any of the same issues. If not, talk with your child to be sure she understands how you can be reached on the telephone, what the rules are, and what is expected. Determine whether there is any undue pressure or stress causing your child to "act out." If your child has any special problems, inform the caregiver so understanding can replace inappropriate discipline. When children know their best interests are being considered, they respond more positively. If the upset is caused by placement in childcare and the child is having difficulty adjusting to the changes, find out what is going on. Try to work the issues out. Try to be consistent, reliable, and sensitive to the child who is making the adjustments, being apart from you, with other new children, and coping with what can sometimes seem to be a very long day. Children do get lonely; they might particularly miss a parent or sibling. They can also get upset and frustrated from unexpected problems—just like they do at home.

You can help your child cope with the changes by explaining what to expect at the home or center, talking things over, listening to his feelings, making sure his clothes are easy to put on and take off, that he has friends in the program, and that he gets enough rest and a good breakfast. You want to know the caregiver respects your child, your family's culture and values, and informs you promptly when any problems arise, so they can be handled quickly and easily.

42

‸‸

GETTING INVOLVED IN THE CHILDCARE PROGRAM

"Some of my best friends now are people I met through my son's childcare center."

"She and I worked in the parent cooperative together and I knew we'd be friends forever."

"Come to a reunion of the family childcare home. The kids would love to get together."

Childcare is a great avenue for making friends. Seeing other parents and teachers interacting with children gives you a new perspective on what you are doing and ideas about how to do things differently. Get involved in your childcare arrangement—it's a great opportunity for you, as well as good for the children and the center or home.

If you interact with teachers, parents, and also the other children in a friendly way or take part in some activities for the center, the whole center will seem more personal. Your friendliness will contribute to building a good feeling all around.

You can get involved in many ways. Your involvement will be of benefit to you, your child, and the other members of the group as well. Here are a few ideas:

- Spend a few hours at the center or home reading stories, playing games, or cooking with the children.
- Contribute some new decorations for the place—curtains, pictures, or plants.
- Contact other parents to organize a fund-raising event for new equipment and toys.
- Arrange to have a guest, such as a pediatrician, nurse, or community health worker, give a health talk for parents in the evening or on the weekend.
- Give individual attention to a child who may have a special need due to a personal problem.
- Establish a "sitting swap" announcement bulletin board as one way for parents to share with each other.
- Set up a revolving lending-toy library parents can contribute to and share in.
- If space is available, set up a parent lounge or a place where parents can relax, sip coffee, and spend a few moments talking before they leave or pick up their children. A bulletin board nearby helps the exchange of information.

Parent discussion groups offer another way to get involved in the childcare program. Meeting other parents for discussion in informal groups can be valuable to everyone. Just knowing you're not alone in your problems when things are rough can ease a lot of stress.

At a party, you might feel a little ridiculous seeking out someone to talk to about "Batman and my child's problems with nightmares" while others are discussing world affairs. Parents' groups give you a chance to talk about what is on your mind. It's an occasion to exchange information about what concerns you and to help other people. Solving your child's troubles with nightmares might not seem as important as world problems, but it is!

An informal parents' group can:

1. give you new ideas
2. reassure you when things don't work
3. give you understanding and support
4. help you grow

Sometimes parents gather informally, meeting on their own once a week or twice a month. Often centers and co-ops have organized parent groups that meet on a regular basis. Co-ops often set aside a few nights a month for various parent group functions and activities. Centers are usually very responsive to parents' desires to get together. Some provide a leader for the group who has specialized knowledge in family problems. Parent groups in metropolitan areas often offer special courses on all aspects of being a parent.

43

~~~~~~

JUGGLING YOUR RESPONSIBILITIES

Parenthood and work are a difficult combination at times. The stresses can overwhelm anyone. Parents often feel like jugglers with too many balls in the air—finances, home maintenance, food, children's changing needs, personal needs, just to name a few. Like experienced jugglers, parents need balance, efficiency, and timing.

The more successful you are with the lifestyle you choose, the more competent you are likely to be at making arrangements and scheduling, getting things done, being true to yourself, and enjoying your children. These are all things you get better at as you gain experience. Your ability changes and grows.

The amount of time you spend with your child is important, but the way the time is spent is more important. Studies of working mothers versus nonworking mothers show the most important factor in children's emotional well-being and later functioning in society is the quality of the relationship among the mother, father, and child rather than the quantity or amount of time spent together.

You took a major step to balance the elements of a busy life when you figured out your essential goals and priorities. Now begin to schedule your time and establish a new routine. You need sufficient time for each of the following:

1. Maintaining your home
2. Pursuing personal goals
3. Teaching and enjoying your children
4. Reaching out to people for social time
5. Spending time alone for personal business and relaxation

Probably it seems there is not quite enough of you to go around, with all the responsibilities you are juggling. Remember: these can be handled one at a time. You cannot do it all at once; you cannot talk to your child, settle a fight, clean house, figure out your finances, calculate your menu for a week, plan the most efficient shopping route, socialize with friends, and make a phone call all at the same time, though you have probably found yourself trying to. You can become harried, and "harried" quickly can become "nasty." To avoid this you have to take all the time you need to handle each problem as it comes along. Do not try to be "Supermom" or "Superdad" and lose your sense of humor and balance under the strain of responsibility.

To take care of your multiple responsibilities requires efficiency and skill, as does any other difficult job. You will gain those skills in time. Budget time for relaxing, personal enjoyment and growth, nurturing your children, and cultivating friendships, as well as for household routines and work. Long hours of work should be balanced against time for yourself.

Find some form of relaxation and exercise. The time spent is well worthwhile to obtain a balance of fitness mentally and physically. And make room for the ups and downs of life. Some days will work better than others.

You cannot do everything and cannot be everything to all people at all times. Do not feel guilty! Catch yourself when you worry about your child at work, or about your work and your responsibilities when you are at home. You can overcome some of your fears by sharing your feelings with other people who have the same interests and concerns. If you find the stresses in your life overwhelming you, get help in working things out through counseling.

Here are some suggestions to help you make the most of your time.

1. *Create special times.* Spend time with your child regularly, both scheduled and spontaneous. During these times allow no interruptions; make your child feel important. Get to know what is happening to your child. Focus on his or her needs. If your child feels loved, you will feel a lot less guilty about not being around all the time. Some activities to do together can include playing with a board game, doing a craft or hobby, reading stories, preparing a meal or dessert, taking a trip to museums, library or toy store, visiting the zoo or going to another place your child wants to go.

2. *Simplify living.* Have potluck suppers and share cooking and sitting with other parents as a regular part of your life. Make clean-up something everyone in the family contributes to, according to their ability.

3. *Expand your horizons.* Take a course; better yet, take two courses—one for yourself, one to share with your children. Work toward a goal—get that better job, work on something such as a community improvement project that will benefit others, and so on. Express yourself. Find a little time to do what you like to do best.

4. *Support yourself emotionally.* Do not let yourself be argued out of expressing how you feel or what you want. Do not be afraid to ask others, including children and friends,

127

to help out. Everyone can pitch in without having the whole burden yourself.

5. *Take time off.* Do things alone once in a while. Take time for your personal health, physical, and emotional needs. Take time when you get home to relax before preparing dinner. Everyone can participate in helping, each in their own way.

Try to manage a good balance among your responsibilities, socializing, and much-needed rest.

REFERRAL AGENCIES

American Council of Nanny
  Schools
Delta College
University Center, MI 48710
(517) 686-9543

Au Pair/Homestay U.S.A.
1015 15th Street
Suite 750
Washington, DC 20005
(202) 408-5380

Au Pair in America
102 Greenwich Avenue
Greenwich, CT 06830
(203) 863-6123

California Child Care Resource
  and Referral Network
809 Lincoln Way
San Francisco, CA 94122
(415) 661-1714

Catalyst
250 Park Avenue South
New York, NY 10003
(212) 777-8900

Child Care Action Campaign
330 7th Avenue, 18th Floor

New York, NY 10013
(212) 239-0138

Children's Defense Fund
122 C Street, N.W.
Washington, DC 20001
(202) 628-8787

Conference Board
  Work and Family Center
845 Third Avenue
New York, NY 10022
(212) 759-0900

Families and Work Institute
330 7th Avenue
New York, NY 10001
(212) 465-2044

The Governess Agency
4655 Cass Street, Suite 405R
San Diego, CA 02109
(619) 270-8311

International Nanny
  Association
P.O. Box 26522
Austin, TX 78755-0522
(512) 454-6462

National Academy of Nannies, Inc.
3300 E. First Avenue
Suite 520
Denver, CO 80206
(303) 333-NANI

National Association for Family Day Care
725 15th Street, N.W.
Washington, DC 20005
(202) 347-3356

National Association for the Education of Young Children
1834 Connecticut Avenue, N.W.
Washington, DC 20009-1800
(202) 232-8777

National Association of Child Care Resource and Referral Agencies
2116 Campus Drive S.E.
Rochester, MN 55904
(507) 287-2220

National Black Child Development Institute
1463 Rhode Island Avenue, N.W.
Washington, DC 20005
(202) 387-1281

National Coalition for Campus Child Care
P.O. Box 528
Cascade, WI 53011
(414) 528-7080

New Ways to Work
149 9th Street
San Francisco, CA 94103
(415) 552-1000

STATE LICENSING AGENCIES

ALABAMA
Supervisor of Day Care and
    Child Development
50 Ripley Street
Montgomery, AL 36130-1801
(205) 261-5785

ALASKA
Social Service Program Office
Division of Family and Youth
    Services
Department of Health and
    Social Services
Box H 05
Juneau, AK 99811-0630
(907) 465-2145

ARIZONA
Child Care Facilities
701 East Jefferson, 4th Floor
Phoenix, AZ 85034
(602) 255-1272

ARKANSAS
Child Development Unit
    Children and Family Services
P.O. Box 1437

Slot 720
Little Rock, AR 72203
(501) 682-8590

CALIFORNIA
Department of Social Services
Community Care Licensing
    Division
744 P Street
Mail Station 17-17
Sacramento, CA 95814
(916) 322-8538

COLORADO
Office of Social Services
Department of Social Services
1575 Sherman Street
Denver, CO 80203
(303) 866-5943

CONNECTICUT
Day Care Licensing
Department of Health Services
150 Washington Street
Hartford, CT 06106
(203) 566-2575

DELAWARE
Director of Licensing Services
Youth and Family Center
1825 Faulkland Road
Wilmington, DE 19802-1195
(302) 633-2700

DISTRICT OF COLUMBIA
Supervisory Child Care
  Specialist
614 H Street, N.W., Room 1031
Washington, DC 20001
(202) 727-7226

FLORIDA
Department of Health and
  Families
Children, Youth and Families
  Program Office
1317 Winewood Boulevard
Tallahassee, FL 32399-0700
(904) 488-4900

GEORGIA
Child Care Licensing
878 Peachtree Street, N.E.
Atlanta, GA 30309
(404) 894-5688

HAWAII
Department of Human
  Services
Public Welfare Division
P.O. Box 339
Honolulu, HI 96822
(808) 548-2302

IDAHO
Department of Health and
  Welfare
450 West State Street
Boise, ID 83720
(202) 334-5700

ILLINOIS
Department of Children and
  Family Services
406 East Monroe Street
Springfield, IL 62710-1381
(217) 785-2688

INDIANA
Child Welfare Division
  Welfare Department
141 South Meridian Street,
  6th Floor
Indianapolis, IN 46225
(317) 232-4440

IOWA
Department of Human Services
Division of Adult, Children and
  Families
Hoover State Office Building,
  5th Floor
Des Moines, IA 50319
(515) 281-6074

KANSAS
State Department of Health
  and Environment
Child Licensing, 10th Floor

900 Jackson Street, Suite 1001
Topeka, KS 66612-1290
(913) 296-1272

KENTUCKY
Division for Licensing and
  Regulation
275 East Main Street
CHR Building, 4th Floor
  East
Frankfort, KY 40621
(502) 564-2800

LOUISIANA
Department of Health and
  Hospitals
Health Standards Section
P.O. Box 3767
Baton Rouge, LA 70821
(504) 342-5774

MAINE
Child Care Licensing Unit
Department of Social
  Services
State House, Station 11
Augusta, ME 04333
(207) 289-5060

MARYLAND
Office of Child Care Licensing
600 E. Lombard Street,
  Suite 312
Baltimore, MD 21202
(301) 333-0193

MASSACHUSETTS
Director of Licensing
Office for Children
10 West Street
Boston, MA 02111
(617) 727-8996

MICHIGAN
Day Care Licensing
Department of Social Services
Office of Children and Youth
  Services
300 South Capitol Avenue,
  9th Floor
Lansing, MI 48910
(517) 373-8300

MINNESOTA
Department of Human Services
Division of Licensing
444 Lafayette Road
St. Paul, MN 55155-3842
(612) 296-3024

MISSISSIPPI
Child Care Licensure
Department of Health
P.O. Box 1700
Jackson, MS 39215-1700
(601) 960-7504

MISSOURI
Department of Social Services
Division of Family Services
Licensing Unit

133

P.O. Box 88
Jefferson City, MO 65103
(314) 751-4279

MONTANA
Program Officer
Department of Family
    Services
Box 8005
Helena, MT 59604
(406) 444-5900

NEBRASKA
Early Childhood Licensing
Nebraska Department of Social
    Service
P.O. Box 95026
Lincoln, NE 68509-5026
(402) 471-9205

NEVADA
Child Care Services Bureau
505 East King Street,
    Room 606
Carson City, NV 89710
(702) 885-5911

NEW HAMPSHIRE
Division of Public Health
    Services
Bureau of Child Care
    Standards and Licensing
6 Hazen Drive
Concord, NH 03301-8584
(603) 271-4523

NEW JERSEY
Bureau of Licensing
Division of Youth and Family
    Services
CN 717
Trenton, NJ 08625
(609) 292-1018

NEW MEXICO
Licensing and Certification
    Bureau
1190 St. Francis Drive
Santa Fe, NM 87503
(505) 827-2448

NEW YORK
Bureau of Child Care
40 North Pearl Street
Section 11B
Albany, NY 12243
(518) 474-9454

NORTH CAROLINA
Department of Human
    Resources
Child Day Care Section
701 Barbour Drive
Raleigh, NC 27603
(919) 733-4801

NORTH DAKOTA
Early Childhood Service
    Program
Department of Human
    Services

Judicial Wing, 3rd Floor
600 E. Boulevard Avenue
Bismarck, ND 58505-0268
(701) 224-4809

OHIO
Bureau of Child Care Services
Department of Human Services
30 East Broad Street, 30th
  Floor
Columbus, OH 43215
(614) 466-3822

OKLAHOMA
Programs Administrator
Licensing Services
Department of Human Services
P.O. Box 25352
Oklahoma City, OK 73125
(405) 521-3561

OREGON
Children's Services Division
Department of Human
  Resources
198 Commercial Street, S.E.
Salem, OR 97301
(503) 378-3178

PENNSYLVANIA
Department of Public Welfare
Bureau of Child Day Care
  Services
P.O. Box 2675
Harrisburg, PA 17120
(717) 787-8691

RHODE ISLAND
Department for Children and
  Their Families
610 Mount Pleasant Avenue
Providence, RI 02908
(401) 457-4540

SOUTH CAROLINA
Department of Social Services
Program Quality Assurances
P.O. Box 1520
Columbia, SC 29202
(803) 734-5740

SOUTH DAKOTA
Child Protection
Department of Social Services
700 Governors Drive
Pierra, SD 57501-2291
(605) 773-3227

TENNESSEE
Department of Human
  Services
Citizen's Plaza Building
400 Deadrick Street
Nashville, TN 37248-9800
(615) 741-7129

TEXAS
Department of Human
  Services
P.O. Box 149030
Austin, TX 78714
(512) 450-3262

UTAH
Office of Licensing
Department of Human Services
120 North 200 West
Salt Lake City, UT 84103
(801) 538-4242

VERMONT
Children's Day Care Unit
Department of Social and
    Rehabilitation Services
103 South Main Street
Waterbury, VT 05676
(802) 241-2158

VIRGINIA
Division of Licensing Programs
Department of Social Services
8007 Discovery Drive
Richmond, VA 23233
(804) 662-9076

WASHINGTON
Division of Children and
    Family Services
Mail Stop OB-41

Olympia, WA 98504
(206) 753-0204

WEST VIRGINIA
Division of Human Service
Capitol Complex
Building 6, Room 850-B
Charleston, WV 25305
(304) 348-7980

WISCONSIN
Division of Community
    Services
Bureau of Children, Youth and
    Families
Room, 465, Box 7851
Madison, WI 53707
(608) 266-8200

WYOMING
Department of Health and
    Human Services
Division of Public Assistance
    and Social Services
Hathaway Building
Cheyenne, WY 82002-0710
(307) 777-5994

REFERENCES

Bergstrom, Joan. *School's Out!* Berkeley: Ten Speed Press, 1990.

Binswager, Barbara, and Betsy Ryan. *Live-in Child Care: Complete Guide.* New York: Doubleday & Company, Inc., 1986.

Broad, Laura, and Nancy Butterworth. *The Playgroup Handbook.* New York: St. Martin's Press, 1974.

Long, Lynette, and Thomas Long. *The Handbook for Latchkey Children and Their Parents.* New York: Berkeley Books, 1984.

McCullough, Bonnie Runyan, and Susan Walker Monsom. *401 Ways to Get Your Kids to Work at Home.* New York: St. Martin's Press, 1981.

National Association for the Education of Young Children. *How to Choose a Good Early Childhood Program.* Washington, D.C.: National Association for the Education of Young Children, 1984.

Navara, Tova. *Playing It Smart: What to Do When You're on Your Own.* Hauppauge, New York: Barron's Educational Series, 1989.

Olds, Sally Wendkos. *Working Parents Survival Guide.* Rocklin, California: Prima Publishing, 1989.

Rogers, Fred. *Going to Day Care.* New York: G.P. Putnam's Sons, 1985.

Swan, Helen, and Victoria Houston. *Home After School: A Self-Care Guide for Latchkey Children and Their Parents.* New York: Prentice Hall Press, 1985.

Yeiser, Lin. *Nannies, Au Pairs, Mothers' Helpers-Caregivers, The Complete Guide to Home Care.* New York: Random House, 1987.

SUGGESTED EQUIPMENT FOR PRESCHOOL PROGRAMS

The review of the physical facility will be easier if you use this guide of suggested equipment.

OUTDOOR EQUIPMENT
balls
climbers
sandbox
sawhorses
slides
swings
tricycles
wading pool
wagons
wheelbarrows

SAND/WATER PLAY
collections of cars, boats, etc.
hose
large plastic dishpans or tubs
large, smooth tin cans, pots, and pans
pails

shovels, scoops, spoons
sifting screens
small dishes (metal or plastic)
sprinkling cans
straws and paper cups

CARPENTRY
hammers
nails with large heads
saws
soft pieces of wood
workbench

GARDENING
flower pots
plot of ground
seeds
small shovels
sprinkling cans
trowels

GENERAL
assorted blocks
books
barrel or tunnel to climb
  through
clock
counting beads
globe
gym mats
magnetic alphabet board
magnets
maps
pull toys
punching bag
steps and platform
Nerf balls
toy cars, trucks, and boats
variety of toys and games

HOUSEKEEPING
areas for playing house,
  grocery store
brooms and dustpans
chests for storing equipment
clothesline and clothespins
cooking utensils
dishes
dolls
doll beds
doll carriages
doll clothes
dress-up clothes/costumes
empty food cartons
ironing board and iron
play furniture
stuffed animals
telephones (dial)

toy carpet sweeper/vacuum
  cleaner
washtubs and washboards

MANIPULATIVE PLAY
dominoes
handlooms and yarn
lacing boards
Legos
needles with large eyes
nested blocks
pegboards
puppets
puzzles
remnants of material
thread or colored yarn
wooden beads or macaroni
  and strings

MUSIC
bells
cymbals
drums
music books
record or tape player
records or tapes
rhythm sticks
tambourines
triangles

CRAFT ACTIVITIES
blunt scissors, paper, and
  wastebaskets
bulletin board or clothesline
  and clothespins for
  display of paintings
chalk and chalk board

colored modeling dough
coloring books
easels
finger paints
jumbo crayons in individual
   boxes
markers
newsprint
paint and paintbrushes
paper cups
paste
pencils
plain paper, construction
   paper
shelf paper for finger
   painting
small jars
stencils

FURNISHINGS

chairs, one for each child
clock
colorful window shades
cots with washable covers
   and light blankets or mats

dishes and equipment for
   meals
fire extinguishers
first aid supplies
mirrors
mops, pails, brooms,
   dustpans, dusting and
   cleaning cloths
needles, thread, safety
   pins
paper towels
pictures, plants
Scotch tape
screens or low movable
   shelves to separate
   quiet areas from play
   areas
small tables with washable
   tops
soap
storage for supplies
thumbtacks
tissues
toilet paper
wastebaskets

QUESTIONS AND ANSWERS

1. By the year 2000, how many mothers with children under ten are expected to be in the workplace?
It is estimated that more than 75 percent of all mothers with children under the age of ten will be in the workforce.

2. What are the different auspices that provide childcare?
Childcare services are available through unions, employers, cooperatives, schools, churches, government agencies, private companies, and individual caregivers.

3. What are the three most common types of childcare arrangements?
In-home caregiver, family childcare home, and childcare center.

4. What are some household responsibilities children can perform?
As children become able, they can learn to put away their toys, books, and clothing. They can clear and set the table for meals and participate in simple food preparation.

5. What are some benefits of childcare for children?
Childcare can assist the child in learning, getting along with other children, developing new skills, learning about other cultures, and gaining self-confidence.

6. What are some disadvantages of childcare?

Childcare can be difficult for some children. They may have trouble adjusting to separation, and they may not feel comfortable in an all-day program away from their familiar surroundings. Children form attachments and can become upset if there is a change of childcare provider.

7. How can you help your child adjust to going to childcare?

You can help your child adjust to childcare by providing gradual experiences with new adults and children, by explaining about the time away ahead of time, and by having a positive attitude about childcare yourself, and by teaching your child appropriate self-sufficiency skills such as how to get dressed and how to tie shoe laces.

8. What are some questions to ask to tell if a childcare situation meets your child's needs?

Will my child be comfortable, secure, and fit in? What are the staff attitudes, training, and expectations? How much individual attention does my child need?

9. What features should you look for in infant care?

You should look for a small number of infants per caregiver; warm, affectionate, well-trained caregivers; and a clean and safe place that is designed for infants. Licensing is important.

10. What is the meaning of a license for childcare?

A license means a childcare program meets the health and safety regulations of your state. States vary greatly, though, in the minimum standards they set for childcare.

11. What should staff training include?

Training should include courses in child development and

child psychology, and specialized courses including behavior problems, nutrition, health and safety, first aid, and use of toys and playthings.

12. What is the average cost of childcare?

The cost of childcare varies from $3 to $6 or more an hour or from $1500 to $5000 or more per year. Experienced nannies may charge $2000 or more per month.

13. What are some activities children do in childcare?

The usual activities include play, meals and snack time, learning activities, story-time, naps, arts and crafts, and cleanup.

14. What are some of the important qualities to look for in a caregiver?

Child caregivers should have a variety of personal attributes and skills. They should be fair, flexible, positive, patient, able to listen to children, have a good sense of humor, respond to children appropriately, be healthy, and emotionally stable.

15. What are some of the different staff involved in childcare services?

Childcare services can include volunteers, social workers, psychologists, health care workers, architects, and a board of directors in addition to the staff and director.

16. What are some important questions to ask when interviewing a potential caregiver over the phone?

Do you have space available, do you have a current license, how many adults work in your program, how many children are enrolled, what are the ages of the children, and how much do you charge?

144

17. What are some of the specifics to look for in any program?

Any childcare program you consider should include appropriate bathroom facilities, a clean play area and rest area, childproof electric sockets and fixtures, a comfortable and cheerful environment, adequate supervision, a nutritious and balanced menu, ample and varied educational and play materials, and a well-trained, qualified staff.

18. Where are some places to locate a caregiver?

Some of the places to check for childcare services include state licensing agencies, childcare information and referral services, nanny agencies, classified ads, the Yellow Pages, friends, bulletin boards, local colleges, schools, and community groups.

19. What terms should you include when considering employing an in-home caregiver?

Consider hours, salary, social security, vacations, insurance, when payment will be made, and the duties expected.

GLOSSARY

Au pair a caregiver who lives in your home and receives room, board, and sometimes a modest salary, in exchange for childcare services.

Caregiver a qualified person who cares for children in your home, her home, or in a center (also referred to as a childcare provider).

Childcare center/home a place where children are cared for during part or for the whole day; also called daycare center, preschool center, early childhood program, full-day nursery school, and Head Start.

Childcare provider *see* caregiver.

Child development the stages by which a child grows from infancy through adolescence, including physical, mental, social, and emotional growth. Understanding each level of the child's growth is essential for caregivers.

Child/staff ratio the number of children being cared for by one adult, as required by regulatory agencies. The ideal child/staff ratio is different for each age group.

Co-op a type of parent-shared childcare program where each parent participates part of the time in some facet of the program. Usually, parents share in actually caring for the children; however, in some co-ops, the parents get together and hire a staff to look after the children.

CPR a first aid technique for cardiopulmonary resuscitation, vital to know for anyone who takes care of children.

Drop-in a "part-of-the-day" childcare program operated by the hour as a special service. Drop-in centers are available in some shopping centers, tennis and health clubs, hospitals and clinics, colleges and universities, and other facilities of this type.

Early childhood education a college curriculum that prepares people to teach young children. Coursework covers child development, teaching methods, classroom management, group games, children's literature, and supervised teaching experience.

Family childcare home as the name implies, a family childcare home refers to care provided in a homelike atmosphere. The children may be the same age or they may be a mix of infants, toddlers, and preschoolers.

Flex-time staggered work hours allowing parents to participate in their children's daytime activities.

Head Start a government-sponsored preschool program offering full and part-day arrangements for disadvantaged four-year-olds.

Latchkey children children who do not regularly participate in any after-school organized program under adult supervision, and are home alone when school is out for the day.

Licensing the authorization given by a state regulatory agency to a childcare home or center, signifying that the childcare service has met state standards.

Nanny a person who cares for your child in your home. Usually, a nanny has had special training and has received either a college degree in child development or early childhood education or a certificate from a nanny-training program.

Playgroup an informal cooperative operated and organized by parents.

Provider *see* caregiver.

Referral agency an agency that provides information about childcare programs available in the community.

Shared-care a childcare arrangement made between an in-home caregiver and two or more families. The in-home caregiver takes care of the children in the home of one of the families. The cost of the caregiver is shared by the families.

Sliding fee scale a flexible fee payment plan to accommodate different parents' ability to pay for childcare.

INDEX

BARRON'S MAKES IT EASIER TO HELP WITH POTTY TRAINING....

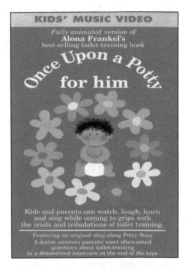

Uh Oh! Gotta Go! Potty Tales from Toddlers

Written by Sesame Street personality, Bob McGrath, Uh Oh! Gotta Go! features 27 humorous vignettes of kids and their potty challenges. (Ages 1–4)

Hardcover, 0-8120-6564-6, $5.95, Can$7.50

Books/videos may be purchased at your local bookstore, or by mail from Barron's. Enclose check or money order for total amount plus sales tax where applicable and 18% for postage and handling (minimum shipping charge $5.95). Prices subject to change without notice.

Once Upon a Potty Videos
Story by Alona Frankel

These amusing, musical, 30-minute videocassettes feature both his and hers versions to direct at your little boy or girl facing the challenges of potty training. (Ages 1–4)

Hers – 0-8120-7701-6, His – 0-8120-7702-4, both $14.95, Can$19.95

Barron's Educational Series, Inc.
250 Wireless Blvd.
Hauppauge, NY 11788
Visit us at our web site at:
www.barronseduc.com

In Canada:
Georgetown Book Warehouse
34 Armstrong Avenue
Georgetown, Ont. L7G 4R9

(#38) R 3/03